CASSELL CARAVEL BOOKS

1. KNIGHTS OF THE CRUSADES
2. HEROES OF POLAR EXPLORATION
3. NELSON AND THE AGE OF FIGHTING SAIL
4. ALEXANDER THE GREAT
5. RUSSIA UNDER THE CZARS
6. CAPTAIN COOK AND THE SOUTH PACIFIC
7. JOAN OF ARC
8. EXPLORATION OF AFRICA
9. SHAKESPEARE'S ENGLAND
10. MARCO POLO'S ADVENTURES IN CHINA
11. THE VIKINGS
12. CAESAR
13. THE FRENCH REVOLUTION
14. CORTES AND THE AZTEC CONQUEST

A CASSELL CARAVEL BOOK

THE FRENCH REVOLUTION

By the Editors of

HORIZON MAGAZINE

In consultation with

PROFESSOR DAVID L. DOWD

Department of History, University of Florida

ILLUSTRATED WITH PAINTINGS, DRAWINGS,
AND DOCUMENTS OF THE PERIOD

Cassell • London

First published in Great Britain 1966
Printed and bound in Italy by Arnoldo Mondadori Editore

MUSEE CARNAVALET

FOREWORD

When the French Revolution was at its height, in March of 1794, a group of Vermont gentlemen met and drank a toast to the new republic of France: "May the success of the brave sans-culottes speedily relieve all the noble souls oppressed by tyranny and break every link in the chain of despotism throughout the world."

Who were those revolutionary Frenchmen, those "sans-culottes" (men without fancy breeches) who stormed the Bastille, who extended their nation's borders by defeating the best armies of Europe's monarchs, and who survived, and even prospered, amid the cruel excesses of the Terror? They were by no means the frenzied, mindless mob portrayed in most fictional accounts of the Revolution—accounts which have generally tended to favour the gentle aristocrats. Rather, they were clerks and tradesmen, lawyers and goldsmiths, bakers and merchants: a crowd of fighting patriots, not a rabble.

Such a three-dimensional picture of the sans-culottes has emerged from modern scholarship and is presented in the narrative on the following pages. It is supplemented by art of the period, not only in the formal, classical works of masters like Jacques Louis David but in the reportorial sketches of individual revolutionaries made on the scene.

In their contemporary enthusiasm, the Vermonters toasted the sans-culottes as global freedom fighters—which they were not. The Revolution that they carried out was not an end but a beginning of the struggle for freedom that is still being fought by courageous men and women in many lands.

THE EDITORS

The artist of this view of Paris worked in the Louvre, directly above the rooms of the painter David. In the scene are the Conciergerie prison (far left) and the Left Bank homes of many sans-culottes across the Seine.

Ragged but enthusiastic volunteers like the one at right were the backbone of France's revolutionary army.

PHOTO ROGER-VIOLLET

COVER: *On August 10, 1792, the people of Paris storm the Tuileries and overthrow the Bourbons.*

MUSEE DE VERSAILLES

FRONT ENDPAPER: *The grim Bastille has fallen, and the governor, Launay, is captured by the mob.*

MUSEE CARNAVALET

TITLE PAGE: *This badge of a Parisian elector bears the proud legend "Liberty—Equality 1792".*

MUSEE CARNAVALET

BACK ENDPAPER: *Royal insignia are burned in a ceremony celebrating the constitution of 1793.*

MUSEE CARNAVALET

CONTENTS

MUSEE DE VERSAILLES: PHOTO GIRAUDON

Versailles Palace, even in this early view of 1668, was an imposing sight. The original hunting lodge forms the centre of the main block of buildings.

DECISION AT VERSAILLES

April, 1789: a blazing beginning to a hot summer. The fields were parched, and the roads leading into the little town of Versailles, some twelve miles from Paris, were clogged with clinging yellow dust. The town, usually a quiet place, was filled with commotion and clamour. Day after day, dust-coated men on weary horses clattered into the streets, stage coaches unloaded their crumpled, irritable passengers at the doors of inns, and elegant carriages with coats of arms on their doors scattered the pedestrians with arrogant speed. For the first time in 175 years, the king of France had summoned the elected representatives of his people—the Estates-General—to meet within the shadow of his palace at Versailles.

The Bourbon kings had built the palace as a monument to their power and wealth. For more than a century, succeeding monarchs had added to its magnificent riot of halls and galleries, apartments and state rooms, terraces and courtyards, making it the wonder of Europe.

Around the main buildings stretched smooth green lawns broken by sweeps of gravelled drives and avenues of stately trees. Fountains splashed and sparkled at every hand. Man-made lakes and Dutch canals mirrored the sky, their placid surfaces broken only by the passage of swans or of gondolas filled with lolling courtiers.

In 1682, King Louis XIV—the Sun King—moved his court to this magnificent setting, and the palace became the gilded prison of the French nobility. Stripped of power by the Sun King, they passed their lives in idle luxury, supported by pensions and grants from the royal treasury and by the income of their vast estates. And while they frittered away the hours in empty court ceremonial, in intrigues and scandals and gambling, Louis ruled as a despot, aided only by a council of state. However, his successors lacked his strength and will—and his able finance ministers. Louis XV was an amiable nobody, and his grandson, who succeeded to the throne as Louis XVI in 1774, was the last and the least of the Bourbon despots. Under his weak and wavering rule, the French aristocrats at last rose in rebellion.

Since the king reigned without a legislature, the only weapon in the hands of the nobles was the thirteen *parlements*, or high courts, whose members were all aristocrats. The *parlements* had to register all royal decrees in their records before they became law; by withholding their approval, they were able to offer some resistance to the king and his council of ministers. In 1759, the *parlement* of Rouen called upon the king to summon the legislature, which had not met for over a century. "Give us back our precious liberty," they demanded. "Give us back our Estates-General." The appeal was taken up by the other *parlements* and repeated in aristocratic manifestoes and pamphlets; the king's ministers were attacked with increasing violence. But the demand for liberty fell on deaf ears. The king clung short-sightedly to his power, where a more statesmanlike monarch would have found a compromise.

But Louis XVI had neither the personality nor the intelligence to control a kingdom or crush a revolution. He was an honest and easygoing man, devoutly religious and painfully shy, and like all the Bourbons, he was grossly fat. Sheer size made him awkward and clumsy, and a clownish fondness for practical jokes made him the laughing stock of his court. He was devoted to his family, but he found it difficult to make friends, and he shunned the company of others. He found peace in his workshop, where he made and repaired locks like a common artisan, or in his library, dabbling in mathematics. But his one great passion was hunting; it was a black day for the king when he failed to make a kill.

Harmless though these qualities were in an ordinary man, they were fatal shortcomings in a king. He never bothered to hide the fact that affairs of state bored him, and the virtues of Louis the man often proved to be vices in Louis the politician. His amiability became indecision; his honesty made him narrow-minded and incapable of compromise; his shyness made him hard to reach. He did not understand people, and his lack of judgment led him to rely on untrustworthy counsellors. He found it difficult to concentrate on the dull business of government, and when a decision was forced on him, he frequently wavered, torn

These three figures are wearing the costumes prescribed for deputies to the Estates General. Above is the commoner, whose simple black suit appears fitting for a prosperous gentleman. By contrast, the aristocrat (centre) and the clergyman (left) wear elaborate outfits that mark them as members of the first and second estates.

by the opposing views of the advisers on whom he depended. And all too often, when he had made up his mind, he would change it again without warning. At the same time, he could be disastrously pigheaded about hasty decisions. For Louis believed that he ruled by the will of God, in an age when such ideas were being attacked and discarded. Isolated in his great palace, he was out of touch with the new ideas that were sweeping through France and with the changing needs and fears and hopes of his subjects.

Twenty-six million Frenchmen lived under the rule of this awkward, indecisive king. They were divided into three orders, or classes, known traditionally as estates. The most important of the three was the rebellious nobility of the second estate. Numbering only some 400,000, these privileged gentlemen held all the public offices in the kingdom: only aristocrats could hold high ranks in the army and navy; only aristocrats were appointed to important posts in local governments; only aristocrats sat in the *parlements*. Most of the king's ministers of state were of noble birth, and even the highest offices of the first estate, the clergy, were filled with the younger sons of noble families. But these were empty privileges. The nobility wanted real power.

The least influential of the estates, the third, was easily the largest since it encompassed every Frenchman who was neither an aristocrat nor a clergyman. It consisted of the middle class—some one million strong—and the vast working class of twenty-four million peasants and labourers.

While the first two orders enjoyed many advantages, the common people had none. Barred by law and by custom from any kind of political power, they were also burdened with taxes. They paid taxes on income, on land, on property, and on their crops; on salt, on tobacco, on wine, and on cider. They even paid a poll tax for the privilege of having been born. The peasant suffered even more than the middle-class citizen. If a peasant sold a piece of land, he paid a sales tax on the money he received, plus an additional tax on the sales tax. Further, he had to provide free labour for the Crown and for the local lord, usually ten days a year. He was forbidden to kill any game animals, even those that came out of the woods to destroy his crops, and the army took his sons for six years' service just when they had reached manhood. For the peasant, France had barely moved out of the feudal world of the Middle Ages.

It is not surprising that the common people joined with

BIBLIOTHEQUE NATIONALE: SERVICE PHOTOGRAPHIQUE

the aristocrats to demand change. The peasants wanted relief from their ancient and out-of-date duties; the middle class wanted freedom as a reward for their industry. Yet Louis resisted all their demands, although he was in no position to bargain. Two major wars and the upkeep of an extravagant court had drained the royal treasury, and a string of mediocre finance ministers had been unable to refill it. They raised loans that were swallowed up by the repayment of earlier loans. They appealed to the aristocrats to surrender their privileges and pay taxes, but the aristocrats refused to give up anything until the king offered them a larger say in the government.

At last, Louis tried the only course left open to him. He decreed new taxes, although he had no legal right to do so, and the *parlements* refused to approve the measures. Blocked at every turn, Louis called an Assembly of Notables, 144 of the most important men in France—most of them aristo-

Elegant and costly entertainments such as this ball celebrating the birth of Louis XVI's son helped to fill the empty and frivolous lives of Louis' pleasure-loving courtiers.

Political propaganda of all kinds was aimed at the French voters before the country-wide elections of 1789. Pamphlets such as Abbé Sieyès' What Is the Third Estate? *(below at left) stated the case for the middle classes, whose revolutionary ideas had been fashioned by Rousseau's rousing* Social Contract *(right). Royalist propaganda, such as the engraving below in which Louis XVI as a youth is directing field hands like a simple farmer, was less effective. The peasants' miserable plight was bitterly illustrated in the cartoon at left, which shows a gnarled old farmer bowed down under the weight of a priest and an aristocrat (symbolizing the privileges of the first and second estates) while rabbits and birds, protected by unfair game laws, eat his crops.*

QU'EST-CE QUE

LE TIERS-ETAT?

Le plan de cet Ecrit eſt aſſez ſimple. Nous avons trois queſtions à nous faire.

1°. Qu'eſt-ce que le Tiers-Etat? Tout.

2°. Qu'a-t-il été juſqu'à préſent dans l'ordre politique? Rien.

3°. Que demande-t-il? A y devenir quelque choſe.

On verra ſi les réponſes ſont juſtes. Nous examinerons enſuite les moyens que l'on a eſſayés, & ceux que l'on doit prendre, afin que le Tiers-Etat devienne, en effet, *quelque choſe.* Ainſi nous dirons:

ALL: BIBLIOTHEQUE NATIONALE: PAMPHLETS, PHOTO ROGER-VIOLLET; DRAWINGS, SERVICE PHOTOGRAPHIQUE

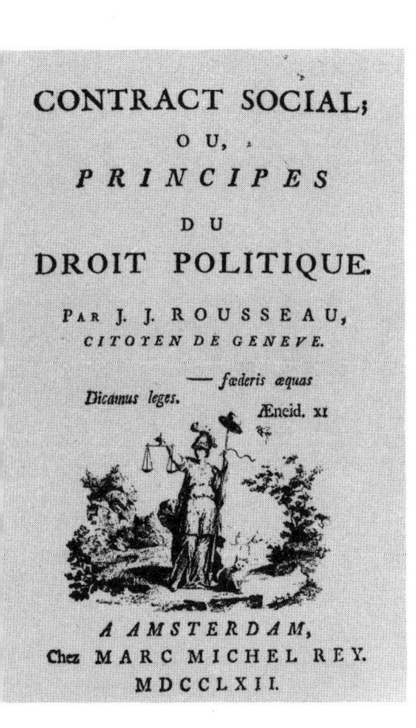
CONTRACT SOCIAL;
OU,
PRINCIPES
DU
DROIT POLITIQUE.
PAR J. J. ROUSSEAU,
CITOYEN DE GENEVE.
— *fœderis æquas*
Dicamus leges.
Æneid. XI
A AMSTERDAM,
Chez MARC MICHEL REY.
MDCCLXII.

crats. He appealed to them for help and received the same answer: no taxes without change. One of the notables, the young Marquis de Lafayette, the recently returned hero of the American Revolution, suggested once again that the Estates-General be summoned, since it alone had the power to create new taxes. But Louis had reigned far too long without a popular assembly, and he refused to yield. He hurriedly dismissed the Notables, only to find that the Paris *parlement* had returned to the attack.

In a fury, Louis ordered the arrest of two of its members and exiled the rest to a small town in the provinces. A storm of protest arose from the nation. Sullenly, the king surrendered to the popular rebellion. He recalled the magistrates and consented to summon the "free and general estates", although he insisted that they meet at Versailles rather than at Paris because he did not want to miss his hunting.

The *parlement* returned to Paris in triumph in September, 1788. It recorded the royal decree summoning the Estates-General for May 4, 1789, adding that the new assembly should be modelled on the last Estates-General, which had been held in 1614. At this, the commoners realized that they had been betrayed by the nobles. For under the old regulations, each estate of three hundred deputies had one vote apiece—which meant that the Third Estate would bc outvoted two to one by the aristocrats and the clergy.

The king's wily finance minister, Jacques Necker, saw at once that he could use the common people's resentment as a check on the ambitions of the nobles. He persuaded Louis to double the number of deputies in the Third Estate, increasing it from three hundred to six hundred, so that it equalled the other two combined. Almost overnight the king and his minister became popular idols. Even when some clear-sighted critics pointed out that nothing had been said about doubling the Third Estate's *voting power*, the people still believed that Louis and Necker were on their side.

This political excitement only increased the popular tension in the weeks before the elections, for France was in a troubled period. Food riots broke out in many places. Rainstorms and hail had ruined the harvest of 1788, and grain became scarce. Many farm labourers were thrown out of work, and during the bitter winter they drifted into the towns in search of food and shelter. Local councils had to keep bonfires blazing in the streets to prevent the poor from perishing of the cold. Gangs of starving brigands roved the countryside, burning and looting. And the common soldiers, angered by the betrayal of their fellow peasants, began to murmur against their aristocratic officers.

At the same time, men's minds were being roused by a flood of political pamphlets. Most of them reflected the revolutionary theories of the eighteenth-century philosophers such as Jean-Jacques Rousseau, who held that a king ruled not by the will of God but by the will of the people. This startling idea had been the basis of Thomas Jefferson's Declaration of Independence, and many Frenchmen had fought in America to make that independence a fact. Now they wanted to bring to France the same freedom that their American comrades enjoyed. Their manifesto was a pamphlet written by a priest, Abbé Emmanuel Sieyès, entitled *What Is the Third Estate?* It answered its own question —"Everything." "What has it been until now?" it asked again. "Nothing." "What does it demand?" "To become something." And it was to make something of that cause that the newly elected deputies of the Third Estate were traveling along the dusty roads to Versailles in the scorching April of 1789.

One of the deputies, the Baron Malouet, was later to write, "No assembly ever contained so many remarkable men." This was certainly true of the representatives of the Third Estate. They were drawn from many different backgrounds and from many professions. The Abbé Sieyès, even though he was a priest, took his place as a deputy from Paris; the Count of Mirabeau had been elected by the people of Aix, although he was a nobleman.

Over half of the deputies were lawyers, like young Maximilien Robespierre, an attorney from Arras who was soon to make a name for himself. A quarter were businessmen and civil servants. The rest were farmers, landowners, scholars, soldiers. In fact, the only class not represented in this array of talents were the unlettered, tongue-tied workers and peasants who had placed their fate in the hands of these intelligent and educated men of the middle class.

Yet even these remarkable new legislators found that their expectations had been raised too high. They had not been long at Versailles before they discovered that they were still considered an inferior body. Following the tradition of earlier Estates-General, they were forced to wear dull black clothes, while the aristocrats blazed in gold-embroidered silks, nodding plumes, and velvet capes, and the prelates of the First Estate gloried in scarlet and purple

MUSEE CARNAVALET

The meeting of the Estates-General was recorded not only in the annals of French history but in the most ordinary everyday things. The fan at top is decorated with a painting of the opening session of the legislature, with Louis presiding on his throne at centre. The pot above bears a satirical design showing the spade of the Third Estate outweighing the bishop's crook of the Church and the sword of the nobility in the balance of politics.

MUSEE CARNAVALET: PHOTO BULLOZ

vestments and fine lace. And at a royal reception two days before the assembly opened, the commoners were kept waiting for hours while the king gave a private audience to the gaudy aristocrats.

But they had their revenge during the opening ceremonies on May 4. A day of pomp and pageantry began with a procession of the court and the deputies from the Church of Our Lady to the Cathedral of St. Louis. Versailles was on holiday. Rich tapestries hung from the houses lining the parade route, and the streets were strewn with carpets. From early morning, festive spectators had poured into the town to crowd the roadsides, the roofs, the windows, and the special stands that had been built in the cathedral square.

At last, between ranks of ramrod-stiff Swiss and French guards, the procession moved out of the church. To the sound of trumpet, fife, and drum, the royal family and members of the court marched slowly through the streets, preceded by ranks of palace officials, mounted pages, and royal falconers with hooded hawks on their wrists. Then came the deputies, carefully separated into their three estates. The resplendent nobles passed by without raising more than a murmur from the crowd, but as the black-costumed commoners came into view, they were greeted with a roar of applause that was ample repayment for the indignities they had suffered.

Early on the following day, the Estates-General settled down to business. The deputies and the hundreds of eager spectators gathered to hear the opening speeches in the gallery that had been set aside for their meeting. Once again, the Third Estate was forced to wait in the corridors outside until the aristocrats and the clergy had been seated by the royal master of ceremonies. Even then, they still had plenty of time, since the king did not arrive until one o'clock.

Among the spectators were the king's brothers, the Count of Provence—Monsieur, as he was known officially—and the Count of Artois, while his cousin, the Duke of Orléans, sat with the deputies. Monsieur was a typical Bourbon, as fat as Louis but unlike him in every other way. He was cunning, ambitious, and frustrated, for there was no room for advancement at Versailles. He despised his dull-witted older brother, and he was one of the busiest intriguers at a court that specialized in intrigue. Artois was an arrogant, feather-brained rake. A wild gambler, he was forever in debt, from which he was rescued by the king's generosity. He was a braggart and a trouble seeker who made enemies more easily than friends, and he was loathed by the common people. He had a high opinion of himself as a statesman, and he constantly tried to force his narrow-minded views on Louis. Luckily, the king chose to ignore his advice, for Artois was easily the stupidest of a family that was not noted for brains.

Orléans combined the worst traits of both of the king's brothers. It was rumoured that he wanted to replace Louis and that he employed spies to stir up the people against the king. He supported the popular outcry for reform more to irritate the king than from any political conviction, and he was twice banished to his country estate for his trouble. He courted the favour of the people by distributing money and food during the winter famines, but his charity rarely stretched to paying his debts.

Orléans must have been disappointed at the cheerful applause that interrupted the king's opening speech. Yet, although they applauded with a will, the audience was left confused; Louis cautioned the deputies to be wise and moderate in their debates and urged them to vote his much-

MUSEE DE PICARDIE, AMIENS: PHOTO BULLOZ

MUSEE DE VERSAILLES

The most stubborn resistance to the Revolution came from the royalist cliques at Louis' court. Foremost among these groups was the Austrian Committee led by the Count of Artois (left) and Marie Antoinette, who were hated by the people for their extravagance. The lavish firework display below, held at the queen's Petit Trianon Palace, was typical of the costly diversions with which they amused themselves.

needed taxes with as little delay as possible, but he did not even mention reforms. However, his audience consoled themselves with the thought that their hero Necker was still to speak. They sat impatiently while the king's chief councilor, Barentin, mumbled his way through a speech that no one heard—or wanted to hear—in the echoing hall.

At last, Necker rose to deliver his statement. Assisted from time to time by a clerk who relieved him when his voice became hoarse, he ploughed through a maze of facts and figures that took three hours to read. At the end of it, the deputies had grasped only two things: that the nation was deep in debt—which surprised no one; and that if they tried to oppose the royal will, they would be dismissed. The subject of reform had been passed over without a word.

Most of the audience refused to believe that Louis and Necker had wilfully betrayed them. It was the queen, they told themselves, who was responsible—she was not called Madame Deficit for nothing.

This was the least offensive nickname that the French had invented for their foreign queen. Marie Antoinette was hated by the people, and she returned their hatred with interest. Her childhood had been spent in the chilly atmosphere of the Austrian court, where she was brought up by her strait-laced mother, Empress Maria Theresa. Married at fifteen to the slow-moving Louis, she soon learned to despise her clumsy husband, and turning to the gay life of Versailles and Paris, she became fast friends with the debauched set that surrounded the Count of Artois. Before long, she was a leader of fashion, adding to the problems of Louis' heavily burdened treasury by her extravagance.

Necker (standing) shows the king how to conceal the size of the deficit from the estates by sleight of hand. Above him, a list of royal loans, headed "New ways to revive France", totals "Deficit". This cartoon appeared early in 1789.

With motherhood, she at last abandoned the giddy round of plays, balls, horse races, and scandal, and turned instead to meddling in affairs of state. She managed to antagonize almost everyone at court and most of the king's ministers. She provided her spendthrift cronies with pensions and had Necker dismissed when he protested (although he was later recalled by a desperate Louis in 1788). She persecuted her enemies with such success that almost everyone was convinced that Louis was under her thumb. So the Austrian Woman, as her people also called her—for she never made a secret of her preference for the land of her birth—became the undeserving scapegoat for many of her husband's blunders, while he continued to enjoy the tolerant affection of his subjects.

Their tolerance had been stretched to the breaking point by the events of the opening session of the Estates-General. The king's action in doubling the Third Estate now appeared as an empty gesture. The commoners could still be outvoted unless the other two estates agreed to a vote by head count. Naturally enough, the aristocrats refused. They were as determined as their middle-class opponents to control the Estates-General.

The deputies of the Third Estate were in a sullen mood when they met on the second day of the session. The other estates had already assembled separately and had settled down to business, but the commoners decided that if they could not win their point, they would do nothing else. They elected Jean Sylvain Bailly, a well-known astronomer, to preside over their meetings, and that was as far as they went. They held no debates, they cast no votes, they did not discuss taxes, they did not even open their mail. And they rejected an attempt by the clergy to reconcile them with the equally stubborn aristocrats. For five weeks they held out, and by the middle of June, their patience was rewarded. The poor parish priests, who were more in sympathy with the Third Estate than they were with their own aristocratic superiors, began to desert the First Estate in ever-increasing numbers.

On June 17, the Third Estate adopted a motion proposed by Abbé Sieyès and declared itself a "National Assembly", capable of acting on behalf of the whole kingdom, since its members were "the only representatives legally and publicly recognized . . . by almost the entire nation". In a stroke, the Third Estate had assumed the power of all the estates, and to protect themselves, the deputies further decreed that taxes were only to be paid while the National Assembly remained in session.

MUSEE CARNAVALET: PHOTO BULLOZ

"All that is needed for harmony is patience" reads the caption on this medal. The optimistic design shows the three estates working together to draw the king in the chariot of state to the Temple of Happiness.

Louis' plan to divide the Estates-General by playing on its rivalries had failed. Instead, he found himself in a difficult situation. If he accepted the National Assembly, he would be surrendering his power; if he opposed it, he might drive the Third Estate to further rebellion. Urged on by the queen and his brothers, and ignoring Necker's warnings, he chose opposition.

On the hot wet morning of June 20, the members of the new Assembly found the doors of their chamber locked and barred, with royal troops standing guard. A note, belatedly sent to Bailly by the king, explained that the hall had been closed for alterations, but the worried deputies suspected something more serious. They were justified. The king was hoping to prevent them from meeting while he completed his plans against them.

Standing in the rain, the deputies debated what they were to do. Some wanted to demonstrate under the king's windows; others favoured a protest rally in front of the palace. Then a certain Dr. Guillotin suggested that they continue their discussion in an indoor tennis court nearby, and the deputies set off through the muddy streets, followed by a crowd of spectators and supporters.

The tennis court was a high-ceilinged hall with walls painted black so that players could see the ball. The first-comers had soon snatched up the few chairs, and President Bailly stood up on the only table (see page 26). Try as he might, he could not control his excited colleagues. At times there were more than a hundred angry men on their feet, waving for attention and attempting to make themselves heard above the din. Finally, towards the end of the day, order was restored, and Bailly read out a motion in the form of an oath, which the Assembly approved with but one dissenting vote. Known to history as the Tennis Court Oath, it read: "The National Assembly . . . decrees that every member . . . shall take a solemn oath not to separate . . . until the constitution of the realm is established on firm foundations." This was an act of open defiance, for it implied that the deputies had met to enact constitutional reforms, and that Louis' taxes would have to wait until they had settled these problems.

Louis replied quickly. He decreed that the three estates should meet for a Royal Session, at which he would preside, three days later.

The deputies arrived on the morning of June 23 to discover the hall surrounded by soldiers. Spectators were to be barred, and the king was to be the only speaker. Necker had opposed the rest of the king's council when they approved Louis' plan. He had warned the king to move cautiously, but true to character, Louis dug in his heels. The finance minister finally offered his resignation in protest, but it was refused, for as the wily Artois pointed out, they needed the popular minister as a hostage.

The king should have listened to Necker. His speech to

BOTH: MUSEE DE VERSAILLES

In 1774 Louis XVI, at the age of twenty, succeeded his grandfather to the French throne. Five years before this—and a year before his marriage to Marie Antoinette—he sat for this portrait by Louis Michel Van Loo, the nephew of Louis XV's official court artist.

the rebellious deputies was an ill-advised attack on their actions. Louis vetoed the National Assembly and ordered the estates to return to the traditional systems laid down by law. He warned the deputies that if there was any more talk of a new constitution, the estates would be dismissed.

With this, he swept from the hall, followed by the members of the Second Estate and most of the clergy. But the men who had sworn ". . . not to separate until the constitution [was] established" remained in their seats. Before long, the king's master of ceremonies returned to repeat the king's order.

The Assembly's answer was delivered by Mirabeau, who had appointed himself spokesman for the rebels. "Tell your master," he bellowed at the startled official, "that we are assembled here by the will of the people, and that we will leave only at the point of a bayonet!"

Louis could not bring himself to use force, and before he could find another solution, it was too late. A stream of clergymen and a large group of liberal noblemen joined the defiant Assembly. The king bowed before the will of the people and ordered the remaining deputies to do the same. Forcibly united by the rebellious middle class, the three estates began to work on a new constitution for France.

The Revolution was in full flood.

Marie Antoinette's portrait was also painted in the year before her marriage, by the French artist Ducreux. Brought up at the Austrian court under the strict discipline of her mother, Maria Theresa, Marie still sought her counsel long after becoming queen of France.

The bedlam that marked the swearing of the Tennis Court Oath is missing from this carefully posed official version painted by the Revolution's leading artist, Jacques Louis David. He was more interested in faces than in facts, and

LOUVRE: PHOTO BULLOZ

he succeeded in creating a portrait gallery: Sieyès sits at the table on which Bailly stands, reading the oath; Mirabeau strikes a dramatic pose in the right foreground; and Robespierre, in the group behind Sieyès, clutches his breast.

II THE TURBULENT CITY

MUSEE CARNAVALET: PHOTO BULLOZ

On July 14, the king wrote in his hunting diary the one word "Nothing" and went to bed. It had been a dull day. But in Paris, only twelve miles away, July 14 had been filled with the sound of guns, and the streets had run with blood.

Paris had always been the storm centre of France. Its narrow streets, crowded with ancient tenements, merchants' houses, churches and palaces, foundries and wineshops and stores, housed a motley population of half a million citizens who were always ripe for trouble. Many of them were the workers from the factories, workshops,

After the king's troops left Paris, citizens' patrols like the one below kept order in the city streets.

From his perch at the Palais Royal (above at centre), one of the many orators who roused the crowd on July 12, 1789, addresses a group of citizens carrying wax busts of Necker and the Duke of Orléans. Camille Desmoulins (opposite), an unemployed lawyer who was among the speakers, was later credited with sparking the Parisian revolt that ended in the fall of the Bastille.

breweries, and tanneries; most were independent artisans and craftsmen or small shopkeepers; and in the better districts lived the wealthy merchants, bankers, factory owners, and professional men.

Since the Paris *parlement*'s triumphant return in September, 1788, the city had seethed with excitement. The Revolution had been the main topic of conversation wherever people gathered: in the boulevards and taverns, in the gardens of the Tuileries Palace, in the arcades of the Palais Royal, which had once been the home of the Duke of Orléans.

Orléans had been forced to turn his beautiful town house to profit in order to pay off his vast debts. He had built arcades around its spacious gardens to house shops,

cafés, and gambling dens, and before long, the Palais Royal was the favourite resort of Parisians of all classes. Here they met to drink a glass of wine and to hear the outdoor orators preach revolution, while in the taverns and cafés, political discussions became heated arguments as ideas clashed over the coffee cups and wine glasses.

Hunger contributed to the tension in the city. The bread shortage, brought on by the bad grain harvests of the previous year, made the situation desperate. All the city's supplies had to be brought in from the surrounding countryside, and before the grain convoys could reach the Paris markets, they were often robbed of their precious loads by starving peasants. Bread riots broke out during the early summer of 1789, and cavalry were called in to bring them to a halt.

The working class of Paris suffered most, for their wages did not keep pace with the sharply rising food prices. In April, at the height of the food riots, they vented their anger on a wallpaper manufacturer who was falsely accused of saying that the French worker was not worth his wages by wrecking his factory and his house. When troops arrived to restore order, they were met with a shower of stones, tiles, and broken furniture, and they fired back, killing many of the rioters.

The commotion reached its peak in early July when units of the king's Swiss Guards marched into the city and went into camp on the Champ de Mars, the parade ground of the military college. Rumours spread that the aristocrats were going to put a stop to the Revolution by armed force.

The rumours were—for once—almost right. However, it was not the aristocrats but the king who had summoned the troops. Although he had given way before the defiance of the Third Estate, he had not surrendered. Backed by the counter-revolutionary party at court—the Austrian Committee as it was called, because it was led by the queen—Louis had called up seventeen regiments of Swiss and German mercenaries and stationed them near Paris and Versailles. He had been forced to rely on foreign troops because he no longer trusted his French soldiers. Only recently the crack French Guards, who formed the Paris garrison, had refused to fight against their compatriots and had been imprisoned in their barracks. Now the king was preparing to fight against the Assembly.

He made his second move, and his second mistake, on July 11. He had chosen the time carefully; it was a Saturday, and the Assembly was not in session. He dismissed his

MUSEE MUNICIPAL, CHARTRES: PHOTO GIRAUDON

council of liberal ministers and sent secret orders to Necker to leave France at once, telling no one of his dismissal. Then he appointed a new council of counter-revolutionary royalists.

News of Necker's fall reached Paris on the following day and sparked the Parisians like a match in a barrel of gunpowder. Angry crowds filled the streets, and at the Palais Royal, where a huge throng had gathered, speakers climbed onto tables and chairs to harangue them. One of the speakers who sounded the call to arms was an impoverished young lawyer named Camille Desmoulins. "The Swiss and German battalions are going to murder the people of Paris," he cried. "To arms, to arms!"

The crowd was joined by the mutinous French Guards, who had broken out of their barracks. Together they rushed into the streets to search for weapons. One group took busts of Necker and Orléans from a museum and paraded them around the city. Another broke into the storehouse of the Tuileries Palace and removed a collection of ornamental guns and some cannon given to King Louis by the king of Siam. Sixty barrels of gunpowder were found

Riots and strikes against low wages marked the early months of the 1789 Revolution and had to be put down by force. Below, troops fire on a mob of rioting workers who are wrecking the factory at far left.

BIBLIOTHEQUE NATIONALE: SERVICE PHOTOGRAPHIQUE

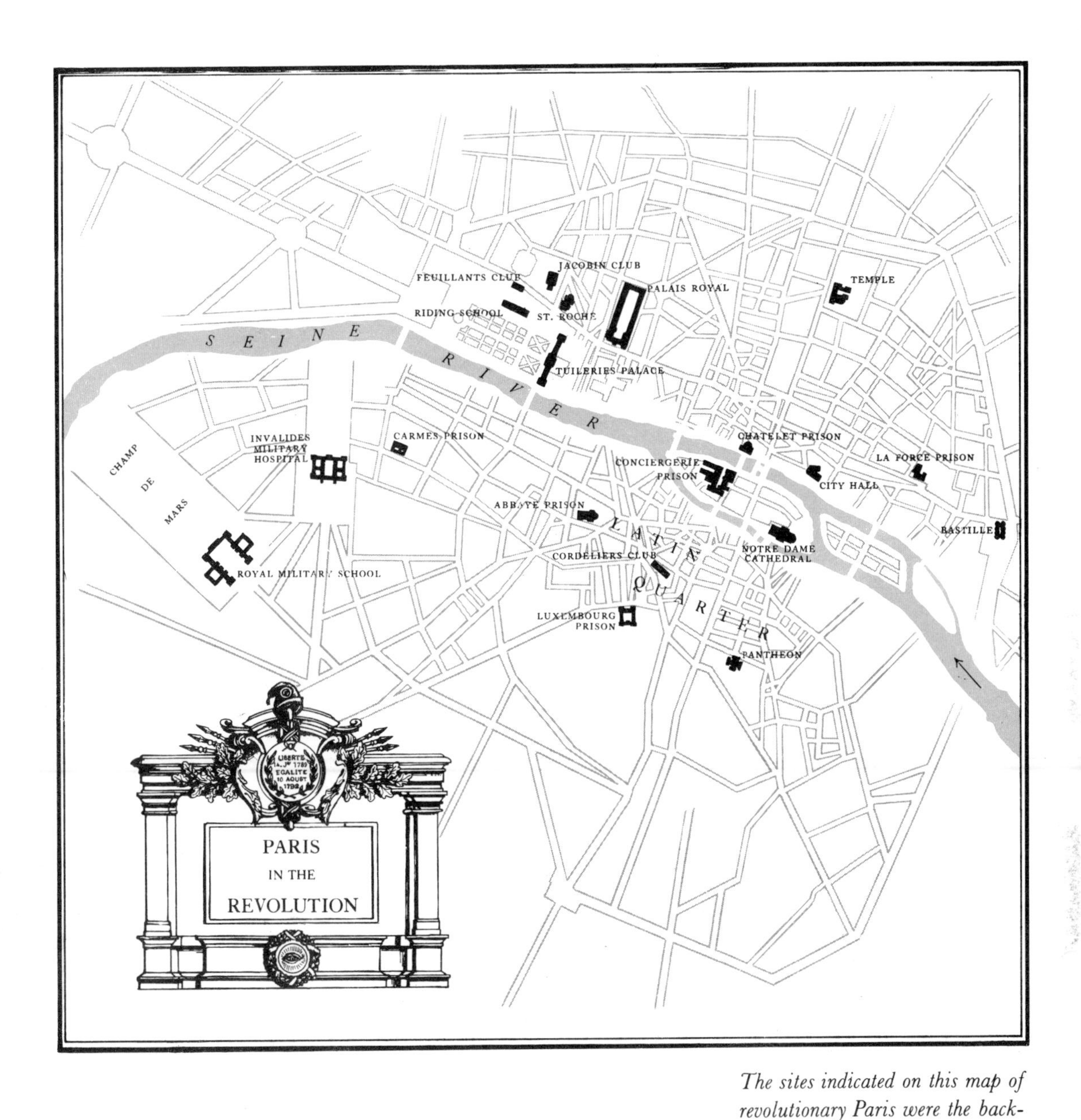

The sites indicated on this map of revolutionary Paris were the background of some of the crucial acts of that turbulent and exciting era.

in a ship in the Seine, and the monastery of St. Lazare was stripped of a supply of grain laid in by the monks. Cavalry patrols clattering along the streets were stoned by the mob, and several soldiers were wounded. They were finally withdrawn by Baron Besenval, the military commandant of Paris, when a squadron of horsemen charged the crowd near the Tuileries Gardens and was driven back by a shower of rocks. Besenval did not want a riot to turn into a civil war because of his actions, and he still had no orders from Versailles.

The rioting went on far into the night and soon got out of

TEXT CONTINUED ON PAGE 36

OVERLEAF: *Paris, with its narrow winding streets and jumbled buildings, looked like a medieval city on the eve of the Revolution.*

MUSEE CARNAVALET

TEXT CONTINUED FROM PAGE 33

hand. The customs barriers around the city were put to the torch, and many shops were looted and burned. On the following morning, July 13, the electors of Paris met in the city hall. They set up an emergency committee to replace the city government, which had failed to meet the crisis, and called for volunteers to form a civil militia for the protection of life and property. In a matter of hours thousands of men had answered the appeal, and before long, patrols, stiffened by regular troops of the French Guards, were moving through the streets, restoring calm to the city.

MUSEE CONDE, CHANTILLY: PHOTO GIRAUDON

Armed only with a pike and a stout cudgel, one of the newly recruited citizen militia performs duty as a garde-blés, *or "harvest guard".*

Finally, the electors sent a messenger to the Assembly to ask the influential Bailly, the Assembly's first president, to accept the position of mayor, and the popular Lafayette to take command of the militia.

Again on July 14, there were fresh outbreaks of violence. As far as the Parisians were concerned, the city was still in danger of being overrun by foreign troops summoned by the aristocrats. Part of the mob seized thirty thousand muskets from the military hospital, the Invalides, when the governor refused to hand the weapons over to the emergency committee's deputation. Then, carrying their empty weapons, they marched across the city to join their comrades who had collected at the Bastille prison, where the city's gunpowder supply had been moved for safety.

The Bastille was a fortress whose ninety-foot towers and grim grey walls had loomed over the working-class district of St. Antoine for four centuries. The governor of the prison, the Marquis de Launay, had been ready for trouble since the disturbances had started. His garrison of about eighty pensioners from the Invalides, reinforced by thirty Swiss Guards from the military college, was too small to hold the outer works of the Bastille, so he ordered his force to man the walls of the inner courtyard. Here, although they had hardly any food, they were in an impregnable position. They raised the drawbridges, ran out the cannon, and waited to see what would happen.

To those who lived and worked in the district, the Bastille had become a traditional symbol of royal oppression, although in fact it had fallen into disuse. But now, the gaping cannon mouths along the walls posed a very real threat to the peoples' lives and homes, and a scared, angry crowd collected in front of the prison.

Before long, a deputation arrived from the city hall to ask Launay to surrender the gunpowder. Launay refused, politely but firmly. But he did withdraw his cannon to avoid provoking the mob and invited the men to breakfast.

During the rest of the morning and into the early afternoon several more delegations were sent to the Bastille with the same request and received the same answer. At last the mob grew impatient. Two men climbed on the roof of a nearby building and hacked through the chains of the outer drawbridge. The main gates were broken open with axes, and the crowd flooded through. They milled around the gate of the inner defences, calling on the garrison to lower the drawbridge and let them inside. The defenders replied with a volley that sent the crowd reeling back. Soon the steady crackle of musketry rose into the summer air.

At first the besiegers had the worst of the fighting. By three o'clock, more than eighty of their number lay dead on the cobblestones, and as many more had been wounded. Then the tide of battle turned. The city militia and the French Guards arrived, dragging the king of Siam's guns and some cannon taken from the Invalides on the previous day. Under heavy fire from the walls, they pulled the guns into the courtyard and trained them on the inner gate.

In July, 1789, while more orderly citizens looked for arms, the out-of-work peasants who crowded the slums at the edge of Paris rioted and looted. Below, an unruly mob sets fire to one of the hated customs barriers at which taxes were levied on goods entering the city.

MUSEE CARNAVALET: PHOTO BULLOZ

MUSEE CARNAVALET

When Launay saw what was happening, he panicked and decided to surrender. Shortly afterward, even before the cannon had been fired, the besiegers saw a porthole open in the drawbridge and a hand emerge waving a slip of paper. They bridged the moat with a plank, and a pale, consumptive young bookkeeper named Stanislas Maillard dashed across to take the note. It was from the governor, and it read: "We have more than twenty tons of gunpowder, and we will blow up the fortress and the whole neighbourhood unless you allow us to surrender."

Lieutenant Elié of the French Guards, who had taken command of the assault, was willing to accept; he wanted the powder. But the crowd would not agree. They continued to shout "No surrender, no surrender" and went on firing at the walls. However, the pensioners inside the fortress had had enough fighting. They lowered the drawbridge, flung open the gates, and lined up inside with their arms stacked against a wall. The besiegers advanced into the inner court. The Bastille had fallen.

After making the garrison prisoner, the crowd rampaged through the building, breaking down doors, shattering windows, and smashing furniture. The captives were marched off to the city hall where three of them were strung up on a lamp post before their guards could come to the rescue. Three officers of the Bastille were butchered in the streets despite a promise of safe-conduct from the leaders of the mob. Launay suffered the cruellest fate of all. Under heavy escort he was taken as far as the steps of the city hall, but there the crowd overwhelmed his protectors and cut his throat. His head was hacked off and paraded through the streets on a pitchfork.

Late in the evening someone remembered that there were prisoners in the dungeons of the Bastille. The keys of the prison were nowhere to be found. They were still being carried in the victory parade, so the cell doors were forced open. There were only seven prisoners in all: two of these were madmen who were taken to the local lunatic asylum; four more were convicted forgers; and the last was an aristocrat who had been jailed at his own father's request for his vicious and debauched life.

During the night news of the fall of the Bastille reached

On July 12, 1789, royal dragoons made an unprovoked attack on strollers in the gardens of the Tuileries Palace. Although the king's troops were withdrawn after the incident, the Parisians rose in arms against the government.

BIBLIOTHEQUE NATIONALE: PHOTO JOSSE-LALANCE

BIBLIOTHEQUE NATIONALE: SERVICE PHOTOGRAPHIQUE

Above, balanced uncertainly on a plank laid across the moat of the Bastille, Maillard reaches out for the governor's surrender note. The king's diary (left) has the entry Rien, *"Nothing", beside July 14.*

Versailles. A court official woke the king and told him what had happened, but Louis did not seem to understand. "It is a revolt," he said. "No, Sire," was the reply. "It is a revolution."

Obviously the king's plan had collapsed. He could not hope to control both the Assembly and Paris, and for the second time in a month he was forced to bow before the will of the people. He ordered his troops to withdraw, and he recalled Necker from exile. The Count of Artois and other members of the Austrian Committee were disgusted by Louis' surrender and fled abroad to carry on their fight from foreign soil; they were the first of a long list of aristocratic *émigrés*.

The king still had another penance to perform. On July 17 he arrived in Paris to confirm the appointments of Bailly and Lafayette—and to make peace with his rebellious subjects. The new mayor met him at the city gates and escorted him to the city hall along streets lined by militia. Almost all of the citizens turned out to see them pass, many still carrying the weapons with which they had fought three days before, and they cheered Louis enthusiastically. "Long live the king," they shouted. "Long live the nation! Long live Bailly and Lafayette and the electors!" And when the king accepted the new cockade that Lafayette had designed as an emblem of the Revolution—a white stripe for Bourbon between red and blue stripes for the city—they cheered yet again. Louis still had the people's affection even though he had lost their respect.

News of the Bastille's fall gave added strength to the Revolution, which was sweeping through the provincial cities and towns of France. Popular clubs were organized to recruit militia, and everywhere revolutionary councils took over from the local officials appointed by the king. Neighbouring towns and provinces formed federations to resist the aristocrats, who were expected to retaliate any day. And the revolutionaries' fears seemed to be shared by the Assembly, which gave legal standing to the militia and named it the National Guard.

In the countryside the Revolution took on a different form. To the peasants, the Assembly seemed to be doing nothing to solve their problems. Wild rumours began to spread that the aristocrats were marching against them. During July and August, fear of the aristocrats became panic, and in several districts, the peasants rose in arms. Châteaux were looted and burned in an attempt to destroy the records of feudal taxes and duties that the peasants owed to their landlords. Landlords who resisted were killed or driven from their homes, and before long, a second wave of aristocratic refugees was streaming across the borders of France to join Artois and the other *émigrés*.

As the first weeks of August passed, the panic faded. The revolutionaries of the towns sent out their new National Guard to maintain order and protect the precious crops, but the rebellious peasants had succeeded in forcing the Assembly to take action on one of the basic issues of the Revolution—the ancient privileges of the nobility.

On August 4, Lafayette's brother-in-law, the Viscount de Noailles, proposed the abolition of feudal rights, and the Assembly passed the measure in a great burst of revolutionary enthusiasm. Later, when the measure was written into law, its authors retreated a little and demanded that the peasants pay compensation to the landowners for their loss of income. But the Assembly's action carried France from the semi-feudal world of the Old Régime into the freer world of the Revolution.

Meanwhile, work continued on the new constitution, and by autumn of 1789 deputies of the Assembly had laid the

TEXT CONTINUED ON PAGE 44

Launay's severed head, stuck on a pitchfork, was paraded through the streets after he was killed by the crowd at the steps of the city hall.

Beneath the smoke-wreathed battlements of the Bastille, National Guardsmen, French Guards, and armed Parisians press forward to the assault through

the outer gate of the prison. At left is one of the huge cannons from the military hospital; its approach led to the final surrender of the Bastille.

TEXT CONTINUED FROM PAGE 41

foundations of the new France in two important acts.

The first was the Declaration of the Rights of Man and the Citizen, which Lafayette had drafted on the lines of the American Bill of Rights. It stated that "Men are born and remain free and equal in rights", and that "The source of all sovereignty resides . . . in the people." It went on to guarantee the basic rights of liberty, security, freedom from oppression, equal justice, fair taxes, and freedom of speech and thought.

Five weeks later, a decree on the basic principles of government was added. The Assembly made it clear that Louis was no longer the sole ruler of France by dividing the government into the executive (the king), the legislative (the Assembly), and the judiciary (the courts). The same act also curtailed the king's power by forbidding him to make laws. All his decrees had to be signed by at least one member of the Council of Ministers, and most important of all, he could no longer reject the Assembly's laws. He could only suspend them with his veto for four years, and if they were part of the constitution, he could not veto them at all.

Louis was thoroughly alarmed by these measures. He refused to give them his approval, claiming that he had to consider them carefully before he signed them into law. But he spent the time desperately—and vainly—searching for some means of halting the Revolution, only to fall back on his old policy of armed force, the policy that had already brought him to the brink of disaster. He summoned the Flanders Regiment to Versailles.

The soldiers arrived on October 1, and their officers were invited to a dinner given by the king's bodyguard of aristocrats. The banquet took place in the palace theatre. Late in the evening the king appeared with the queen and their son to be greeted with cheers and toasts while the band struck up a royalist air. Amid enthusiastic applause, the diners threw the new tricolour cockade of Paris on the floor and trampled on it as a mark of their loyalty to the king.

This imprudent behaviour aroused the Parisians to fresh anger when it was reported in the city. Conditions had improved little since the fall of the Bastille, and the newly appointed city government—the Commune—which had replaced the emergency committee of the electors, had been unable to improve the food supply. Bread riots had broken out again. Newspapers added to the disorder by spreading rumours that the aristocrats were responsible for the shortage and by urging the Parisians to bring the king to the

MUSEE CARNAVALET

Lafayette designed the best-known emblem of the Revolution, the tricolour (red, white, and blue) cockade. One of these is shown above, pinned to a document decorated with the symbols of the Revolution.

Standing amid a litter of trampled revolutionary cockades, the royal family (left foreground) is toasted by the officers of the Flanders Regiment at the banquet given at the Versailles Palace on October 1.

city, where he would be safe from the plots of the nobles.

On October 5 a crowd of women collected at the city hall after finding no bread in the bakers' shops. They were particularly angry that counter-revolutionaries could hold banquets at Versailles while they went hungry. The Commune could offer them no help, so the infuriated women broke into the building, stole several muskets and some of the city funds, and then set off for Versailles to see what the king could do. They collected fresh groups of marchers on the way through the city and forced passers-by to join them. Young Maillard, the hero of the Bastille, put himself at their head in the hope of maintaining order, and together they stepped out along the highway to the beating of drums under a threatening grey sky.

Lafayette was in a quandary. As commandant of the National Guard he should stop the march—indeed, some units of the French Guards attempted to do so—but his popularity would suffer if he used force against the women. Besides, if the king were brought to Paris, he would be under Lafayette's thumb, and the commandant was an ambitious man. On the other hand, if any harm came to the king, he would be disgraced. For hours he hesitated. Finally his own men forced his hand. They demanded to be led to Versailles to protect their womenfolk and to bring back the king. Toward evening, they moved out in the wake of the marchers.

Meanwhile a heavy rain had begun to fall, and the women pressed on through the mud. Townspeople along their route took shelter behind locked doors and closed shutters. The tough women of the fish markets, who had organized the demonstration, amused themselves by tearing down shop signs, inventing bloodcurdling tortures for the queen, whom they hated, and sharpening their long knives on the milestones. Late in the afternoon, the wet, bedraggled procession wound into Versailles and made for the Assembly.

The royal family—or "the baker, the baker's wife, and the baker's boy", as they were called by the bread-hungry crowd—lead the procession back to Paris in an English cartoon printed not long after the women's march on Versailles.

While Maillard presented their petition for bread to the deputies the women crowded into the public galleries and even sat in the deputies' benches, hanging out their skirts and stockings to dry. They shouted encouragement, advice, and abuse at the speakers and refused to listen to anyone but Robespierre and Mirabeau. All business came to a halt. Finally, a deputation of six women was sent to the palace to see the king, with strict instructions to watch their language. Then a suggestion was made that the demand for the signing of the Declaration of Rights be attached to the women's petition, in the hope that the king would be stampeded into agreeing to both.

At the palace, the king had returned from his hunt and had received the women's deputation with his usual good grace. He gave them a written pledge that he would have grain delivered to Paris. But when the Assembly's deputation arrived, he refused to see them. He made them wait for hours while he racked his brains for a solution to his dilemma. However, there was nothing he could do but submit to their demand. Helplessly, he summoned the deputies and handed them a note promising that he would sign the declaration, but as he did so, tears of rage glittered in his eyes.

However, the king was to suffer still another humiliation before he was allowed to sleep. About midnight, the Paris National Guard stumbled into the town, its rain-soaked banners hanging limply from their poles. Lafayette went to see the king at once and told him that the men wanted to escort him to Paris. By this time the king was exhausted and his resistance was gone. He promised that he would leave the next day. Satisfied, Lafayette pledged that he would protect the king from harm and finally persuaded everyone to get some sleep.

Towards dawn the sleepers were rudely awakened by a din inside the palace. A gang of women and some of the men who had accompanied them on the march had found a way in through an unlocked gate. They spread through the building, intent on finding the queen and murdering her. But the door to her apartment was barred by a courageous servant who held up the would-be assassins long enough for the queen to bundle on some clothes and escape to her husband's room. Here the royal family gathered, expecting the worst.

Outside the palace, the royal bodyguard was fighting the crowd, although, on the king's orders, their pistols were unloaded. Two of them had been killed by the time the National Guard arrived to drive the mob from the palace and restore order.

Lafayette hurried to the king's bedroom to take charge. He persuaded the royal family to move out on the balcony so that the crowd could see them. When the king appeared, he was cheered, but for his wife there were only threats and insults. Dissatisfied with this demonstration, Lafayette led the queen out again and knelt to kiss her hand, showing that she was under his personal protection. He too was cheered. Finally, as the impatient citizens began to shout "To Paris, to Paris", the king returned and repeated his promise to go with them.

About noon the head of a long procession reached Paris, bearing the gory new banners of the Revolution—the heads of the two dead members of the bodyguard impaled on pikes. Then came a stream of dishevelled men and women walking or riding on stolen carts and gun carriages. Unkempt and ragged, they still marched triumphantly; they were bringing back "the baker, the baker's wife, and the baker's boy", as they had christened the royal family, and the promise of bread. The royal prisoners followed behind with an escort of one hundred deputies and the rest of the mob. They reached the city as night was falling, and through the darkened streets of Paris, the royal coach bore them to the Tuileries Palace, which had not sheltered a French monarch for more than a century.

It was a strange homecoming for a king.

These respectable-looking women in their fashionable pleated bonnets were among the rioters who murdered two of the royal bodyguards at the palace. The one on the right holds a pike, the favourite weapon of the revolutionary Paris crowds.

M^{r}. DE LA FAYETTE

Député de la Sénéchaussée de Riom, à l'Assemblée Nationale,
Elu Par Aclamation :
COMMANDANT GENERAL
de la Garde Nationale Parisienne

Dans ces Traitées et dans sa Vie l'Europe connoit son Genie
Regne la droiture et l'honneur Et les Infortunées son Cœur

Constitution et Confédération Nationale
Paris, ce 14 Juillet 1790.

III

FLIGHT TO VARENNES

Marie Joseph Paul Yves Roch Gilbert du Motier, Marquis de Lafayette, had a noble pedigree as long as his name, yet he was the idol of the French people because of his liberal ideas. At the age of nineteen, he had left his native country, against the orders of the king, to offer his services to the American rebels in their fight for independence. He found the glory he had sought under the command of George Washington, who became his friend and his model.

THE AMERICAN NUMISMATIC SOCIETY

Under Washington's influence, Lafayette was converted to the democratic ideas of the American revolutionaries; on his return home, he became one of the earliest champions of the French Revolution. In the Assembly of Notables, he was foremost in demanding a revival of the Estates-General; he drafted the Declaration of Rights for the Assembly; and he was deeply involved in the shaping of the constitution.

Yet there was something cold and unreal about Lafayette's liberalism. It was an ideal, not a code for men to live by; it was more theory than practice. He was not among the aristocrats who had joined the Third Estate to declare a National Assembly, and although his popularity with the common people had made him the most powerful man in the kingdom, he returned their admiration with distrust. Outside the Assembly, he did not mix with his fellow deputies who were members of the Third Estate but preferred the company of aristocrats, and his cold aloofness offended those who might have become friends and allies.

Adulation and applause, both in America and France, had given him a higher opinion of himself than his talents warranted. After the "October days" he conveniently forgot that his men had forced him to go to Versailles, and he

Lafayette (opposite) appears on his famous white charger in a print celebrating his appointment as commander of the Paris National Guard. Louis (above) is less flatteringly portrayed on a gold double louis of 1786.

saw himself as the saviour of the king and the nation. His ideals became clouded by ambition, by a vision of France ruled by the king under a liberal constitution with Lafayette as the real power behind the throne. He began to sacrifice his ideals to this dream. He became suspicious of everyone about him; he became insolent enough to lecture the king and queen on their shortcomings; he began to treat criticism and advice with a high hand. Finally—and fatally—he ceased to care what anyone thought of his actions, and he became a law unto himself.

Bishop Talleyrand, denied a military career by a childhood injury, and forced by his father to enter the Church, was one of the Assembly's most anti-clerical members.

CABINET DES DESSINS, LOUVRE

BOTH: MUSEE DE VERSAILLES, PHOTO GIRAUDON (LEFT)

Two of the Third Estate's leading deputies were the prim lawyer from Arras, Maximilien Robespierre (above at left), and the Count of Mirabeau (at right), whose scandalous habits had made him a well-known personality long before he ran for election in the spring of 1789.

But in October, 1789, he was riding the crest of a wave. He had the affection of the people, the respect of the Assembly, the apparent confidence of the king and queen; France lay in the palm of his hand.

Two weeks after Lafayette had "rescued" the king and escorted him to Paris, the Assembly followed—and lost a third of its members in the move. Three hundred die-hard monarchists who had steadily opposed the reform of the government resigned rather than risk their lives among the rebellious and unruly people of Paris. Most of them fled abroad to join the ever-growing army of *émigrés*. The remaining seven hundred lawmakers soon settled into new quarters in the royal riding school on the north side of the Tuileries Gardens, a mere stone's throw from the palace.

The Assembly was changing. It was no longer clearly divided into those who supported the Revolution and those who did not. It had split into three groups. By far the largest of these was the moderates, whose leading figure was Lafayette. They called themselves the Patriots, but they were more often referred to as the Centre because they sat together in the centre of the assembly hall, opposite the president's chair. The Centre wanted a government in which the king ruled France, the Assembly made her laws, and both were governed and guided by an enlightened, liberal constitution. To the president's right sat the few remaining royalists who wanted to return to things as they had been before the Revolution. And to the left were the extreme revolutionaries, led by the "incorruptible" Robespierre.

These groups were not parties. They had no organization and no set policy, consisting rather of collections of deputies who held the same general views. No one deputy to the Assembly agreed completely with any other, and each one thought that his own ideas were the best. This led to incredible scenes of confusion in the debates since every deputy insisted upon the right to speak his mind on every issue. They loved to hear the sound of their own voices, though only a handful could lay any claim to being orators. It was difficult enough in any case to hear the speakers' words. As they droned off their interminable speeches, their colleagues interrupted or drowned them out with applause, abuse, cheers, groans, and catcalls. And those who were not even trying to listen would wander across the floor of the Assembly or huddle in corners deep in conversation. The public, who crowded the spectators' galleries, added to the din; no one came to the debates simply to listen and watch. Every Frenchman had something to say about the constitution and had no qualms about giving vent to his feelings at the top of his voice.

Despite the confusion, in its first eighteen months in Paris the Assembly managed to pass the measures that were the basis of the constitution. The most important item on the Assembly's agenda was the chaotic financial situation, which it had inherited from the Old Régime. The deputies had been summoned to solve this problem in the first place, and since their first session in Versailles, it had grown into a major crisis. Necker had made two attempts to raise loans and had failed. The Assembly, with equal lack of success, had asked the French people to make the government a voluntary gift of a quarter of their yearly income. And since the August abolition of duties formerly paid by the peasants to their feudal lords, most of the peasants had refused to pay taxes of any kind.

A possible solution was offered by one of the leading clergymen, Charles Maurice de Talleyrand, Bishop of Autun. Talleyrand, like many other French prelates, came from an aristocratic family and had been forced into the Church. He was a minister of religion in form only; at heart he was anti-clerical and an agnostic. Since his election to the Estates-General, he had been shifting to the extremists of the left, and his proposal certainly reflected their views.

MUSEE CARNAVALET

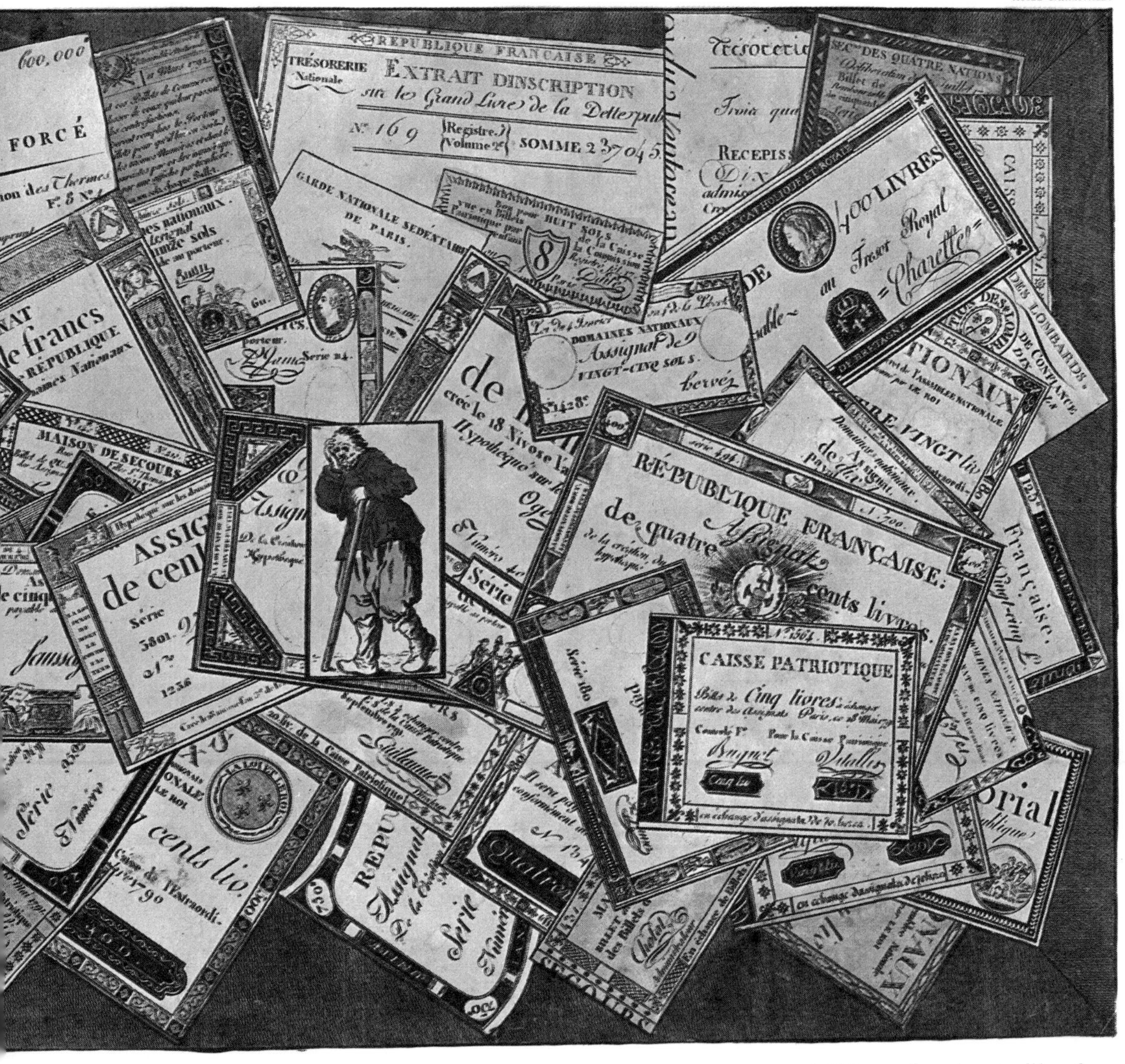

Millions of assignats like those above, backed up by the confiscated lands of the Church, were issued by the revolutionary assemblies in a futile attempt to solve France's never-ending financial problems.

Talleyrand suggested that the nation take over the Church's land and sell it to pay off the national debt. Since the value of Church property in France amounted to more than a quarter of the country's total wealth, there would still be enough left over to support the Church. A howl of protest arose from the high-ranking clergy: they argued that the Declaration of Rights guaranteed the right to hold property. But their protest was in vain. The Assembly had to have money, and on November 2, Church lands were put "at the nation's disposal". And the Assembly also took over the Church's responsibility for education, public charity, and the salaries of the clergy. A

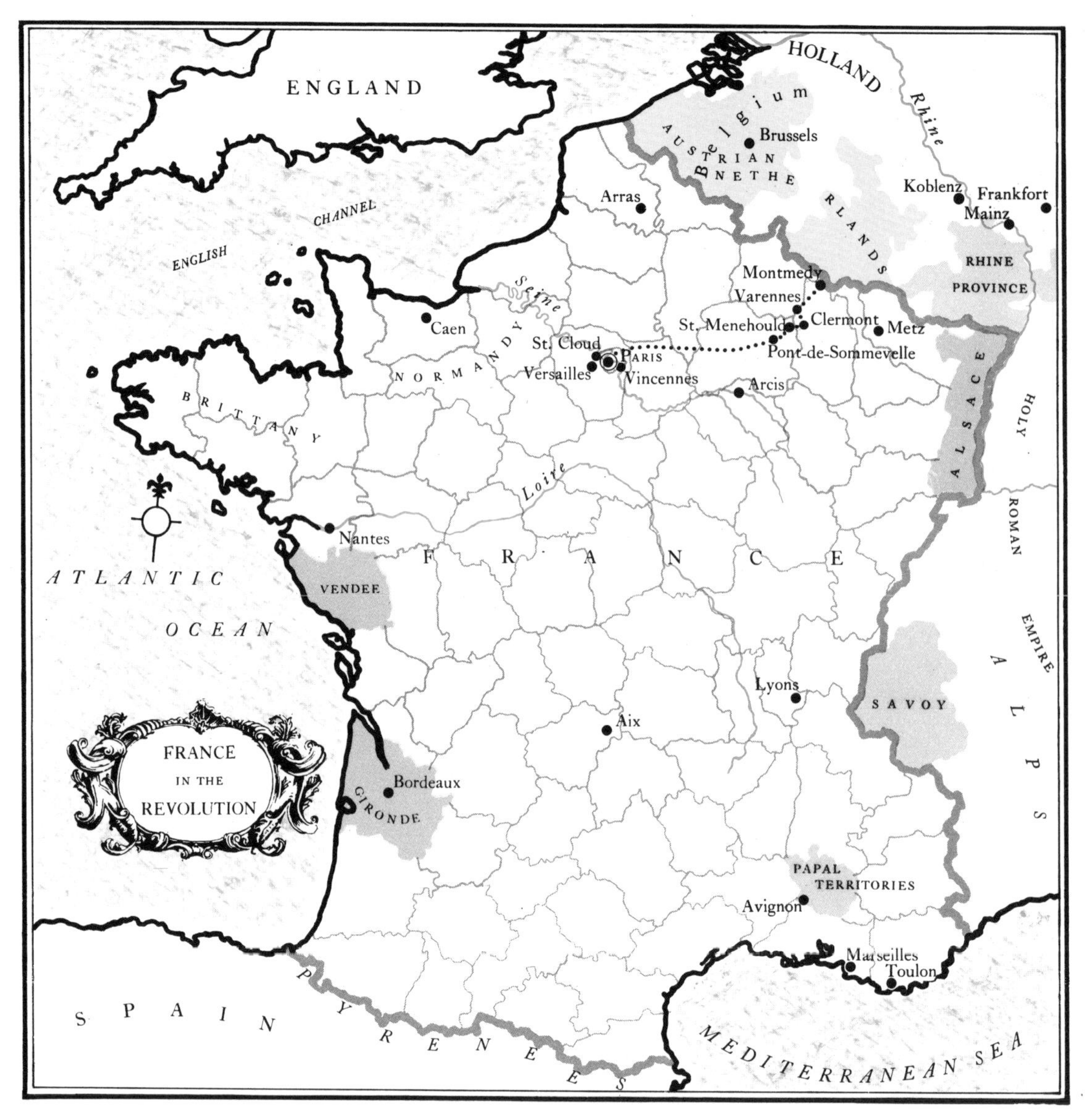

In the map above, light blue areas indicate the Austrian Netherlands, part of Leopold II's Holy Roman Empire and the main theatre of the revolutionary wars. Darker blue indicates areas in which counter-revolutionary forces arose. The areas in grey are territories occupied by France during the Revolution. A dotted line from Paris shows the escape route of the king.

special bank was set up to issue bonds called assignats, which earned an interest of 5 per cent and which the public could buy and exchange for land. Before long, however, so many assignats were issued that they took the place of coins and became France's first paper money.

The Assembly also carried out major reforms in the electoral system. France was divided into eighty-three departments, each one centred on an important town. Each department was subdivided into electoral districts, which were further divided into municipalities, or communes. The vote was given to every man over twenty-five years of age who paid taxes equal to the local value of three days' wages. As in the elections of 1789, these voters elected a board of electors (who had to pay taxes equal to ten days' wages in order to qualify), and they selected the deputies (who had to pay taxes of one silver mark, roughly fifty days' wages).

Each commune, district, and department had its own local government, which was elected in the same way. These local governments were largely independent of the Assembly in Paris. They were set up as a reaction against the Old Régime, when all political power had been gathered into the hands of one man, the king. But in giving so much freedom to the departments, the Assembly weakened its own authority and created many problems that future lawmakers had to face.

Another fault of the new political system was that it widened the breach between the lower classes and the middle class. The "active" citizens, that is, those who paid the taxes and could vote, were nearly all the middle class and the well-to-do peasants; the "passive" citizens, those who did not earn enough to pay the taxes, were mostly the poorer peasants and workers. For them, the golden promise that the Revolution seemed to offer had not yet been fulfilled.

BIBLIOTHEQUE NATIONALE: SERVICE PHOTOGRAPHIQUE

In a scene repeated many times during 1789 and 1790, clerics take the loyalty oath in a village square.

The Assembly did, however, improve the system of justice. All the corruption of the old system—bribed judges, the buying and selling of offices, the preferential treatment of the rich and the mighty—was swept away. It was replaced by freely elected judges, trials by jury, courts of appeal, and free legal counsel for those who could not afford to pay for it. And under the new system much of the savagery of the old courts disappeared: torture as a legal aid was finally abolished, sentences were more merciful, and evidence was examined with greater care.

In July, 1790, the Assembly followed up the decree on the Church's property with a sequel that rocked France from top to bottom. The deputies maintained that since the nation paid the salaries of the clergy, the people should have the right to elect priests and bishops as they did mayors and deputies. The new law put this idea into effect and added that the clerics must swear the same oath of loyalty to the constitution and the nation as other public officials did.

A storm of protest broke on the lawmakers' heads. Most Frenchmen were devout Catholics, and they did not see any connection between revolution and religion. However,

This revolutionary inkstand shows a sans-culotte red bonnet squashing a writhing priest. The top of the bonnet is hinged to make a lid.

the Assembly refused to back down, and in November it passed a second decree that threatened with dismissal those clergymen who refused to take the loyalty oath.

The prelates of France appealed to the Pope for guidance, but he refused to intervene. He held territories at Avignon, in the south of France, and he was afraid he would lose them if he provoked the hostility of the Assembly. Without any support from their spiritual head, the clergy split into two hostile groups. Talleyrand and a handful of bishops, with about half of the priests, took the oath. The rest refused and were dismissed as non-jurors. However, many Frenchmen would not accept the "constitutional" priests, as the oath takers were called. They rallied to the rebel clergy, who became the leaders of counter-revolutionary movements in many parts of France.

During his first year in Paris, Louis had made no open move to turn back the Revolution or to thwart the work of the Assembly. His first attempts to use armed force had failed, and he recognized that less obvious methods had to be used if the monarchy was ever to regain its former power. He made an unspoken truce with the Assembly while he worked secretly on his counter-revolutionary plans, and he watched without protest as the new lawmakers stripped away his privileges. But the loyalty-oath decree—which brought the Church under the control of the revolutionary state—stung him into action. He had surrendered most of his political power, but he refused to compromise with his faith.

At the height of the October riot, the king had almost decided to escape; a carriage had been waiting for him at the door of the palace. What had been a moment's impulse grew into a fixed aim. However, Louis could not make up his mind how or when to escape, or where he should go, or even what he should do if he succeeded. The queen wanted him to go to Austria, raise an army, and return to wipe out the revolutionaries, but the king, in his fuzzy way, was fond of his subjects and could not bring himself to agree. He also felt that if he co-operated with the *émigrés*, they would seize power on their return, and he would simply have exchanged middle-class masters for aristocratic ones. If he called on his brother monarchs to invade, the price he would have to pay later would be heavy. In any case, neither his cousin, the king of Spain, nor the queen's brother, Emperor Leopold II of Austria, showed any sign of wanting to make war on France, although they offered their sympathy. In his dilemma, Louis cast about for aid and advice and received them from the most unlikely source—the Count of Mirabeau.

Mirabeau had been a leader of the Revolution even before his defiance of the king at Versailles. His eloquence and enthusiasm quickly brought him into the limelight, and his fat, short-legged figure with its bloated face, horribly pitted with the scars of smallpox, was a familiar sight in the Assembly's debates. As his influence grew, however, he fell into the same trap as Lafayette; he became too ambitious.

He realized that he could never win control of the Assembly with words alone. He needed the backing of a position of power and tried to win the king's confidence in the hope of being appointed to the Council of Ministers. His hopes were soon crushed by the Assembly. Suspecting his plans, it rushed through a measure that prevented the king from choosing his ministers from among the deputies.

In this print, titled "Revolutionary Ninepins", a patriotic sansculotte prepares to bowl over the monarchs of Europe. Behind him stands Liberty, who holds a victory wreath over him while the many-headed beast of counter-revolution crouches waiting among the rocks.

BIBLIOTHEQUE NATIONALE

Mirabeau's cause was a hopeless one in any case. The queen disliked him for his liberal views, and the king refused to select a man whose life was an open disgrace, for Mirabeau was known as a notorious rake. In his youth he had been jailed several times for his escapades, and he had created further scandal by abandoning his wealthy wife after squandering her fortune.

Each of the sections of Paris had its own flag; the banner of the Cordeliers (above) was unique in that it displayed no royal emblem.

At the same time, Mirabeau also caused a political uproar when after a special mission to the Prussian court he published the secret papers with which he had been entrusted. Not content with this, he wrote several pamphlets assailing the incompetent minister of finance and other members of the royal council. This earned him another prison sentence, and after his release, he fled to England to avoid further trouble with the king.

He returned to France in the early months of the Revolution, still in disgrace at court and still discontented and rebellious. Rejected as a candidate for the Estates-General by the Second Estate, he sought and won his seat as a deputy for the Third Estate of Aix. In May, 1789, he took his place among the commoners.

Now, without any official title but with his sizable debts settled and a handsome monthly salary from the royal treasury, he had become the king's most active counsellor. And both as a deputy and a royal adviser, he earned his pay, deluging the Assembly and Louis with a flood of ideas. He literally worked himself into an early grave, for he died in April, 1791, exhausted by the excesses of his youth and his labours in the cause of the Revolution. His last act, as he lay on his deathbed, was to write the one word "sleep".

Mirabeau's favourite scheme, which the king rejected, as he rejected all of his adviser's plans, was to create a council of ministers consisting of the most powerful men in the nation and to browbeat the Assembly into obedience. Naturally, Mirabeau saw himself as the leader of the group. And Lafayette, naturally, did not see eye to eye with him. Between them Lafayette and Mirabeau might have saved the king, but they could not work together. Mirabeau despised Lafayette's narrow-mindedness and was jealous of his popularity and power; Lafayette was shocked by Mirabeau's scandalous behaviour and envied his talents. And the king, becoming adept at petty intrigues, used their hostility to play them off against each other and to prove to them that no one was indispensable.

During these months of semi-imprisonment at the Tuileries, Louis' mind turned more and more often to the idea of escaping from Paris. But he was unable to conceive a workable plan.

Toward the end of 1789, the secret police uncovered three royalist plots to rescue Louis. The queen's private secretary, who engineered the first, was tried and then acquitted for lack of evidence. The author of the second plot fled abroad before he could be arrested. The Marquis de Favras, who had dreamed up a wild scheme to raise an army in the south and march on Paris, was condemned and executed.

Though the king had not been connected with any of these plots, they endangered his plans because they brought the possibility of his escape to everyone's attention. In order to soothe suspicion, Louis made a speech to the Assembly in which he condemned those who worked against the Revolution and pledged his support to the work of the Assembly. The deputies and the public seemed to accept him at his word, despite the fact that he had already made several attempts to overthrow the Revolution by armed force.

A few weeks later, the king solemnly renewed his pledge during the celebration of the first anniversary of the fall of the Bastille. The Assembly decreed a public holiday, and a massive celebration was planned. Thousands of workmen descended on the Champ de Mars to build stands for the spectators and to erect a huge altar, the Altar of the Nation, in the centre of the parade ground. People poured into Paris to see the celebrations, and detachments of the provincial National Guard, the *fédérés* as they were called, marched into the city from all over France to take part in the parade.

On the great day, the rain poured steadily from early morning on, but it dampened nobody's spirits. Two hundred thousand citizens turned out to see the king and the Assembly walk in solemn procession, followed by the blue-coated *fédérés*. At the Altar of the Nation, Talleyrand said mass—the last he was ever to say—and the king took a solemn oath of loyalty to the nation and to the constitution. Lafayette was there in all his glory to lead the National Guard in pledging their allegiance to the same cause. But while the *fédérés* may have meant what they said, the king's oath was a sham: since the Assembly's decree on the clergy only two days before, he had resolved to escape from Paris.

The queen had finally evolved a plan that had a chance of succeeding. The king was to make his way to the district around Metz, in north-eastern France, where a royalist

TEXT CONTINUED ON PAGE 62

MUSEE CARNAVALET: PHOTO BULLOZ

This wooden statue of a National Guardsman was used to indicate the location of an enrolment centre.

The first anniversary of the fall of the Bastille was marked by a lavish spectacle on the Champ de Mars, present-day site of the Eiffel Tower. Specially built stands held thousands of spectators and gave them a clear view of Talleyrand saying his last mass at the Altar of the Nation (at centre). In the foreground, National Guard units from the provinces march into the arena through a triumphal arch. The king sits at the opposite end of the field on a raised throne (2).

TEXT CONTINUED FROM PAGE 59

general, the Marquis de Bouillé held command of a French army. There, Louis could raise his standard under the protection of loyal French troops; and if his appeal to the nation was unsuccessful, the border of the Austrian Netherlands was conveniently close.

However, the suspicions raised by the Favras plot had not died down. When the king's aunts asked for passports to leave France, the suspicions began to harden into certainty. The belief that the king was about to escape roused the Parisians once again, and they did not hesitate to show how they felt.

A week after the king's aunts had fled to Rome, the Assembly decided to restore the prison at Vincennes, about four miles from Paris, where Mirabeau had served one of his sentences. The attention given to this fortress revived a legend that there was a tunnel leading from Vincennes to the Tuileries. On February 28 a mob of suspicious Parisians marched out of the city, determined to destroy this mythical escape route by storming the prison as they had stormed the Bastille. Expecting an attack on the Tuileries when the mob returned, a crowd of aristocrats, armed with daggers and determined to sell their lives dearly, collected at the palace.

BIBLIOTHEQUE NATIONALE: SERVICE PHOTOGRAPHIQUE

Madame Élisabeth, the king's sister (above), who saved the queen's life by impersonating her during the invasion of the palace in June, was one of the royal party who tried to escape with the help of Marie's favourite, Count Axel Fersen (below).

THE NATIONAL MUSEUM, STOCKHOLM

Lafayette was everywhere at once, with no clear idea of what was the best thing to do. At last he followed the marching Parisians and arrested some sixty of their ringleaders. Then he returned to the Tuileries to arrest several of the dagger-toting aristocrats so that he would not be accused of favouritism. He also took the opportunity to deliver one of his usual lectures on duty to the aged Duke of Villequier, who was responsible for keeping unwelcome visitors out of the palace.

A second incident was even more ominous. Louis had decided to go to his palace at St. Cloud, two miles from Paris, to attend Easter services led by a non-juring priest. This angered the Parisians, who remembered that the king had sworn to uphold the constitution, and, in any case, they were determined that he was not going to leave the city. On the day of the royal family's departure, a mob gathered around their coach as it stood in the courtyard of the palace, and refused to let it move. Lafayette and Mayor Bailly arrived, a little late as usual, and talked to the angry citizens until they ran out of words. No one took any notice. The mob continued to grow, and the people became more sullen. Some of the bolder demonstrators began to rock the coach and shout insults, and at last Lafayette persuaded the king to return to the palace before more serious damage was done.

Louis was furious. He finally made up his mind to adopt the queen's plan, and on Monday, June 21, 1791, the royal family fled from Paris.

The details of the plan had been worked out by the queen's most ardent admirer, the Swedish Count Axel Fersen, who had been sent to Paris as the representative of the king of Sweden. He was a handsome, charming, completely self-satisfied man, and the queen found him attractive and was flattered by his attentions. Fersen, for his part, was supposed to be in love with the queen, though it is doubtful that he loved anyone as much as he loved himself. However, he proved to be a capable intriguer.

The royal family was to travel disguised as the retinue of Baroness de Korff, a German noblewoman who travelled frequently along the route they were to follow. Their destination was a town near Montmédy on the border between France and the Austrian Netherlands (see map on page 54). The Marquis de Bouillé would cover the last part of the journey with troops from his headquarters at Metz,

In the engraving below, an English artist erroneously shows the disguised royal family leaving the palace together on the night of their escape. Leading the party, Louis, dressed as a servant, flashes his lantern on Fersen to identify him.

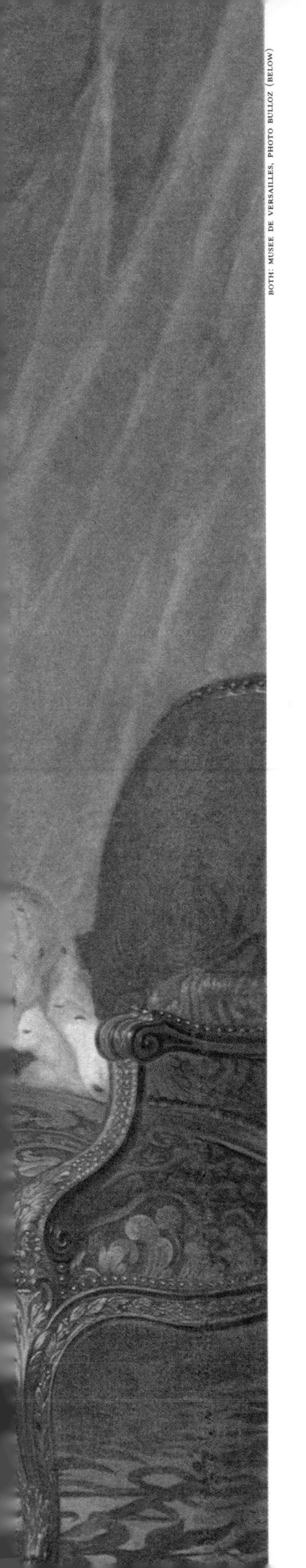

BOTH: MUSEE DE VERSAILLES, PHOTO BULLOZ (BELOW)

fifty miles away, and the Emperor Leopold had promised to mass his army along the border to give Bouillé an excuse for moving up his men.

The guard at the Tuileries had been increased after the king's attempt to leave for St. Cloud at Easter, but one exit, the door to the apartments of the same Duke of Villequier who had been lectured by Lafayette, had been overlooked. This was the escape route. Fersen arrived after nightfall, driving a hired hack and disguised as a coachman. He picked up the royal children and their governess, who was to act the part of the Baroness de Korff. After driving around the city for a time—it was too dangerous to park the carriage close to the palace—he returned for the king's sister, Madame Élisabeth, who was dressed as a maid. Not long after, the king joined the party, and finally, after a breathless wait, the queen arrived. She had lost her way in the darkness. At midnight, already an hour late, Fersen drove the party through the St. Martin gate where

Louis XVI (opposite) seems every inch a king in the portrait by the court painter Duplessis, while Marie appears in a mother's role in the charming painting above, one of more than twenty made of her by Marie Vigée-Lebrun.

MUSEE CARNAVALET: PHOTO BULLOZ

BIBLIOTHEQUE NATIONALE: SERVICE PHOTOGRAPHIQUE

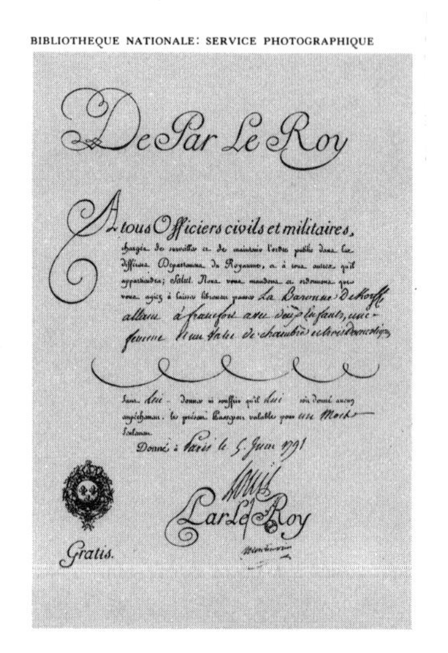
De Par Le Roy

A tous Officiers civils et militaires,

Donné à Paris le 5 Juin 1791

Par le Roy

Gratis.

The passport of the Baroness de Korff (above) was used by Madame de Tourzel, the royal governess, on the flight from the capital. The flight ended when the king was recognized from his portrait on an assignat (at top, in upper right corner) and was arrested.

the passengers transferred to a large, roomy coach in which they were to complete their journey.

Three members of the king's bodyguard had accompanied the royal family. One of them was sent ahead on horseback to make sure that fresh horses were ready at the posting stations along the way. A second rode behind as footman, and when the fugitives were clear of the city, the third took the reins from Fersen, who was to make his escape to Belgium. Louis insisted that the count had already done more than his duty and should not endanger himself further. Fersen rode off into the night with words of affection and gratitude ringing in his ears as the new driver hitched up the reins, released the brake, clucked at the horses, and set the coach rumbling off on the long road toward Montmédy.

All during that day, the royal family jolted its way across the countryside. It was hot, and choking clouds of dust were kicked up by hoofs and wheels, but no one seemed to care. They were free. The king had recovered his spirits, and he entertained his companions by reading them a copy of a statement attacking the constitution and calling for a counter-revolution. He had left the original copy of the document behind for his enemies to find. Even two accidents with the horses, which delayed them further, did not depress him; soon they would all be under the protection of Bouillé's troops. Louis would not have been so confident had he known what was happening on the road ahead.

The first part of the royal escort was a squadron of dragoons that had been stationed in the little town of Pont de Sommevelle. Their commander, the Duke of Choiseul, told the townspeople that the detachment was there to protect Bouillé's pay wagons. But the wagons had passed through the town earlier, and Choiseul's story only aroused angry suspicion. A restive crowd began to collect, and Choiseul panicked. He had expected the royal fugitives at two o'clock. At six, delayed by the late start and the accidents, they still had not arrived, and the crowd was growing more excited and more angry as time passed. At last Choiseul decided to move out before there was a riot, but before he left, he sent a messenger to the other units waiting along the road to inform them that the king would not arrive that day.

Thus, when the royal coach reached Pont de Sommevelle, there was no one to meet it, and at the next stop, a town called St. Menehould, the escort was unsaddled and unready. To make matters worse, the whole district was now in a state of alarm, and the National Guard had been ordered to stand to arms. When the royal coach moved on, the guardsmen prevented the troops from following. The same thing happened at the next stop, Clermont. The plan was going astray. And at St. Menehould the king had been recognized. Jean Baptiste Drouet, the man who was in charge of the posting station there, had identified the king from his portrait on an assignat. He warned the townspeople, and then leaping on a horse, headed across country to cut off the king's escape. He discovered that the king had passed through Clermont and was on the way to Varennes.

At Varennes, Drouet clattered past the royal coach, which had been held up at the outskirts of the town by yet another hitch. There were no fresh horses to carry it on the next stage of its journey. Louis finally managed to persuade the postilions from St. Menehould to take him farther into the town. It was the last mistake he was to make on that fateful journey. At the bridge spanning the river at Varennes, the royal family's flight came to an end. Drouet had roused the mayor and some National Guardsmen, and they had blocked the bridge with overturned carts.

In this English cartoon, entitled "French democrats surprising the royal runaways", a startled king and queen, still disguised, are confronted by a howling mob of citizens of Varennes. As a joke, the artist gave Louis' profile to Marie.

MUSEE CARNAVALET

The royal passengers were forced to alight and were taken to the house of the district attorney, where the governess made a gallant attempt to carry off her part as the baroness, but no one was deceived. The evidence of the portrait was damning; this dust-coated figure, clothed in the drab costume of a servant, was indeed Louis XVI, King of the French. A squadron of hussars, who had been waiting at the town, tried to rescue the king, but they were driven off by the National Guard, and all hope of escape vanished.

The following morning at eight o'clock, the dusty royal coach was turned around, and the long journey back to Paris began.

News of the king's capture was swiftly carried to the Assembly by messengers from Varennes. Lafayette, who had ordered out the National Guard to search for the fugitives, issued a warrant for their arrest, and the Assembly selected three deputies to escort the royal party back to Paris. They found the coach on the day after it had left Varennes surrounded by a triumphal procession of thousands of cheerful citizens who had joined the parade as it made its slow way through the countryside.

The outward journey had taken less than a day; the return took four days. The prisoners were led over a roundabout route so that their captors could exhibit them to as many people as possible. On June 25, as night began to fall, crowds collected in Paris to see the king make his entry. By eight o'clock, as the royal coach passed through the city gates under a heavy escort of cavalry and National Guardsmen, the people had filled the roadsides to overflowing. Many had found places on the roofs of buildings or had climbed into trees along the route to get a better view. National Guard units lined the streets, their muskets reversed as though for a funeral procession, and the waiting throng was hushed.

For the third time they were seeing the king arrive in Paris. The first time, after the fall of the Bastille, he had come of his own free will; the second time, after the march of the women, he had come as the unwilling guest of the people of Paris; now, and for the last time, he came as a prisoner.

Surrounded by masses of National Guardsmen, the coach containing the royal fugitives returns to Paris. Despite the solemnity of the occasion, several industrious pickpockets in the crowd continue to practise their profession.

Vive la Nation

IV

VIVE LA REPUBLIQUE!

Louis was a bad liar at the best of times. When questioned by deputies of the Assembly, he tried to deny that he had meant to leave France, and he swore that he had not intended to obtain foreign troops to quell the Revolution. Yet he could not explain why Monsieur, who had left Paris by a different route on the same night, had continued across the border or why Bouillé's troops had been mobilized. In fact, the more he was questioned about the flight to Varennes, the more Louis confirmed fears that the kingdom of France had lost its king—in spirit, though not yet in person.

MUSEE CARNAVALET: PHOTO BULLOZ

This crisis came at the worst possible time, for the Assembly was seeking to make some significant changes. New elections had been called for; the constitution was almost ready for final approval. The deputies had been working earnestly toward those ends. Moreover, both extreme factions in the Assembly—the monarchists who wanted to return to the Old Régime and the group around Robespierre who wanted a republic—supported a measure disqualifying the present deputies from running for re-election. Each group hoped that it would win more victories at the polls by offering slates with many new candidates.

Then came news of the flight to Varennes, and with that everything was changed. Instead of a quiet, relaxing end to the session, the Assembly was faced with a crisis. Louis had made matters even more difficult by leaving behind him the damning declaration that he had read to his family during their flight. In it he had attacked the constitution item by item and had called on the French people

The attitudes of the early revolutionaries are reflected in the badge above, which combines Bourbon lilies with revolutionary bonnets. But by June, 1792, when an angry crowd invaded the palace and forced the king (opposite) to drink a toast to the Revolution, a more violent and extreme mood prevailed.

BIBLIOTHEQUE NATIONALE: SERVICE PHOTOGRAPHIQUE

BIBLIOTHEQUE NATIONALE: SERVICE PHOTOGRAPHIQUE

A typical sans-culotte (above) is dressed in the uniform of the movement—red bonnet, short jacket, and long striped trousers. Many sans-culottes were members of the Cordeliers Club and carried cards like the one below, which belonged to Robespierre's brother Augustin.

MUSEE CARNAVALET

to rise against the Assembly. Now, those words could not be explained away, nor could the king's subsequent testimony be relied on to ease the fears of the populace.

As an immediate measure to hold the country together, and to get on with their business, the deputies suspended Louis from power until he agreed to sign the constitution and accept his new role as a constitutional monarch. The Assembly also put out the story that the king had actually been captured by Bouillé's agents.

No one was satisfied. Robespierre denounced Louis as a deserter. Others went even further, asserting that the king had abdicated by running away, and the extremists were calling for a republic.

The loudest protests came from the Cordeliers Club, one of the many political societies that had sprung up since the beginning of the Revolution. The club met in an abandoned Cordelier (Franciscan) monastery across the Seine from the Tuileries. Its members were typical sans-culottes—labourers, small businessmen, and artisans—who had organized the Paris crowd into a powerful political force and wore as a uniform the long loose trousers of the worker, not the elegant knee breeches (culottes) of the aristocrats and the well-to-do.

Deprived of a say in the government because they were too poor to qualify as voters, the sans-culottes found a political voice in the Cordeliers. For a fee of a few pence a month, they could gather to hear the tempestuous speeches of the club's middle-class founders: burly Georges Jacques Danton, the originator and first president, who was equally happy trading words or trading blows; nervous little Camille Desmoulins, the hesitant stammerer who had found a steady voice on the day the Bastille fell; Jean Paul Marat, the monkey-faced, bloodthirsty society doctor who had turned journalist to mount a vicious and ceaseless attack on the government; and Jacques Hébert, whose extremist newspaper was infamous for its obscene language. Under the guidance of such headstrong men, the sans-culottes brought pressure on the deputies, who now governed France, by presenting petitions to the Assembly and backing them with threats of the mob violence that the deputies had come to know and fear.

In the space of two weeks the Cordeliers brought before the Assembly two petitions that demanded the removal of the king and the declaration of a republic. Both were ignored, but the idea of a republic received such widespread support that the Cordeliers continued with their efforts. They decided to hold a rally on the Champ de Mars on July 17. The people of Paris could hear what the Cordeliers had to say and could show their approval of the petition by adding their signatures.

On the night before the rally, a group of Cordeliers, seeking aid in other quarters, went to the most powerful of the clubs, the Jacobin. This was basically a debating society where politically minded citizens could air their views and discuss the issues of the day. But many of its members who were deputies, ranging from Lafayette on the right to Robespierre on the left, also used the club as a campaign headquarters where they could organize their forces and plan their tactics.

The power of the Jacobins came from their leadership of a network of hundreds of similar clubs across France.

The candle-lit group below has met for an evening of songs inspired by the Revolution. The most famous of these airs is the rousing marching song of the fédérés, *which later became the national anthem of the French — the "Marseillaise".*

MUSEE CARNAVALET

These clubs were a strong influence in local governments—as the Paris Jacobins were in the Assembly—because they were the strongholds of the middle-class forces that had taken over the Revolution and were shaping its course. Because of the Jacobins' power and prestige, the sansculottes of the south bank were now seeking the support of the Paris club.

The left wing of the club was in favour of joining the rally; Lafayette and his royalist faction were opposed. When they saw that the majority was against them, they resigned in protest and set up a rival headquarters across the street in the exclusive Feuillants Club, which had been started by Lafayette a few months before.

Early on the following day, as the crowd began to drift toward the Champ de Mars for the rally, two men were found hiding under the Altar of the Nation, from which the petition was to be read. Neither could explain why he was there, so they were both hustled off toward the city hall by the police. Before they had gone very far, however, they were seized by the suspicious crowd and lynched.

When word of the incident reached Mayor Bailly, he hurried to the Assembly for help and was advised to de-

Political clubs sprang up in hundreds during the Revolution. The revolutionary debating society pictured below, perhaps the Jacobin Club, is modelled on the Assembly. The president and the clerks sit on raised seats at centre, and the speaker's rostrum is at far left. In front of the clerks' bench is a carving of the Bastille that may be one of those cut from the actual stones of the demolished fortress.

MUSEE CARNAVALET: PHOTO BULLOZ

clare martial law. So Bailly ordered the National Guard to break up the meeting. When Lafayette reached the Champ de Mars, there was no sign of trouble. People were peaceably lined up waiting their turn to sign the Cordeliers' petition; but the leaders of the rally were in an ugly mood. They had just learned that the remaining Jacobins, after an all-night debate, had decided to withdraw their support from the rally.

When Lafayette, as commandant of the National Guard, ordered the crowd to disperse, he was greeted with abuse and laughter. Angrily he repeated the command, and the crowd, becoming equally angry, began to hurl stones instead of insults. Then, somewhere in the mass of people, a pistol barked, and the ball whined past Lafayette's ear. Turning to the blue-coated ranks behind him, he snapped out the expected order. Musket barrels flashed in the sun, and butts slapped into shoulders, hammers clicked back as one, and the National Guard opened fire. Volley after volley crashed into the defenceless crowd.

When the black smoke drifted away, the crowd had scattered like starlings, leaving thirteen dead and many more lying wounded where they had fallen.

The toll of lives was not heavy—seven times as many had been killed under the walls of the Bastille—but the after-effects of the "massacre", as the republican propagandists called it, were tremendous. For a time, the Cordeliers ceased to exist, their leaders hunted by the police. Danton fled to England; Marat found a natural hiding place in the cellars and sewers of the city, where he contracted the terrible skin disease that was to plague him for the rest of his life. The Jacobins too were under a cloud, and Robespierre secretly changed his lodgings in fear of arrest. Lafayette, his popularity gone, was dismissed from his command, and Paris remained under martial law for weeks.

The most striking result of the massacre was its effect on the elections. When the Assembly came to an end on Friday, September 30, 1791—two weeks after the king had signed the constitution and had been restored to power—it was replaced by a body of a very different character.

On the surface, there were few differences between the new deputies of the Legislative Assembly and their predecessors; the electoral laws had made certain that they were all solid, middle-class citizens, and many of them were lawyers. There were, however, no monarchists among them. The conservatives of the right were now the Feuillants, the moderates who continued to follow Lafayette's

MUSEE CARNAVALET: PHOTO BULLOZ

This derisive cartoon of a typical Jacobin shows him as a confident and prosperous member of the upper middle class. In contrast with the sans-culottes, he wears the tight knee breeches of the aristocrats.

Billowing clouds of gun-smoke hide the Altar of the Nation as Lafayette on his white horse leads the National Guard against the crowd in the Champ de Mars massacre.

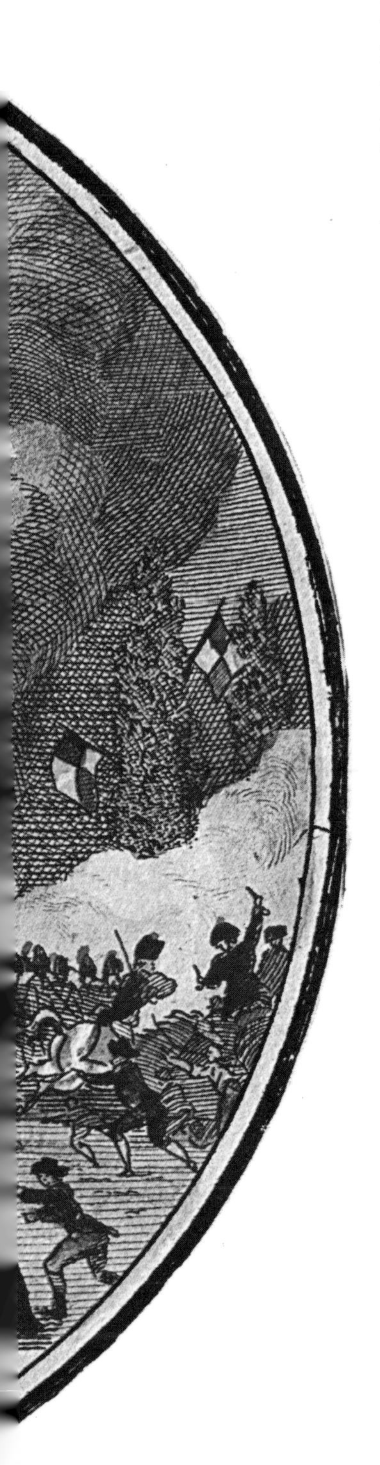

policy of a limited monarchy and who were named after the club that had become their rallying place. The left was made up of a number of groups that had not been seen in the old Assembly. They advocated a republic, and their most extreme wing, which was nicknamed the Mountain because it sat in the raised seats at the end of the hall, represented the sans-culottes of Paris. The new Centre, although few of its members held any strong convictions, generally leaned toward the left, since it had been elected with the help of the Jacobin clubs.

Unlike its predecessor, the Legislative Assembly was served by experienced politicians. Many of the new deputies had been in office for the last two years as mayors, district attorneys, or councillors in the departments and communes. Already in those two years they had become disillusioned with the constitution they were now called upon to enforce. Their discontent was shared by the French people; only one fifth of the qualified voters had gone to the polls.

The Legislative Assembly had to face a host of serious problems. The assignats were rapidly falling in value as speculators, both in France and abroad, forced the price down for their own profit. The *émigrés* helped by flooding the country with forged notes. And as the assignats fell food prices rose. Even the good harvests of 1790 and 1791 had done little to relieve the chronic food shortage. Hoarders kept grain off the market, and greedy merchants exported it while the government was forced to import wheat to feed its citizens. Supply convoys were attacked and robbed before they could reach the warehouses. Soap was in short supply, and sugar stocks dwindled, cut off by a revolt of Negro slaves in the French-held Caribbean islands. Food riots began to break out once more. To add to the Assembly's troubles, royalist ex-deputies seized control of several departments and were conspiring with nonjuring priests to rouse the people against the government; and *émigrés* were training an army of invasion in Koblenz, across the Rhine.

The burden of solving these problems fell on the new leader of the Assembly, a liberal Jacobin deputy from Paris, Jacques Brissot. Brissot headed a loosely knit group of Jacobins whose most important members were deputies from the department of the Gironde. These men, who are sometimes called Girondists, were intelligent, but they shared one common fault: they tended to be idealists and dreamers. Steeped in the works of Rousseau and the great writers of classical Rome, they saw themselves as incarnations of the noble leaders of that ancient republic. But unlike the Roman senators they admired, the Girondists preferred theory to practice. These deputies were not realistic politicians as was their chief opponent, Robespierre. He now controlled the Jacobin Club, which the Girondists neglected to attend or pay much heed to. They gathered instead in the home of Jean Marie Roland, whose domineering, ambitious, shallow wife became their muse, their guide, and their counsellor.

Typically, the Girondists avoided the desperately knotty issues of finances and food shortages and tackled the simpler problem of the counter-revolution, which had been gathering strength since 1789. Within weeks of the elections, they passed a decree that condemned to death any *émigré* who failed to return to France by January, 1792, and followed it with a second threatening the non-juring clergy with prison. Louis promptly vetoed both measures, and the problems still remained unsolved.

MUSEE CARNAVALET: PHOTO BULLOZ

Jacques Brissot, an ex-journalist who had been sentenced to the Bastille for his attacks on the court, became the leader of the powerful Girondist group in the Assembly.

But the Girondists still refused to face the issues squarely. They turned instead to the politician's oldest remedy for internal troubles—foreign war. Without knowing it, they played straight into the king's hands, for Louis had been in constant touch with his fellow monarchs and was still hoping to rouse them to action. If France was invaded, he was sure that the counter-revolutionaries would rally to him; he also hoped that war would help him curb those outspoken *émigrés* who wanted to set up an exclusively aristocratic government. And a threat of war from the French government might turn the scales and persuade the European powers to attack first.

So, for entirely different reasons, the king and the Girondists found an issue they could both support. They soon had the people behind them. The old fear of the aristocrats was never far below the surface, and the Girondists handled their propaganda skilfully. They preached a crusade against the tyranny of the European kings; the French people were persuaded that it was a duty to spread abroad the liberty they had won for themselves. Only the voices of Robespierre and Danton rose against the enthusiastic clamour. They read the minds of the king and their opponents in the Assembly, and they guessed that Lafayette would certainly be recalled from retirement. But their protests were drowned by the voice of the people. All that remained was to find an enemy and an excuse for war.

Austria, the traditional foe and the homeland of the

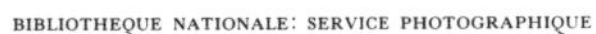
BIBLIOTHEQUE NATIONALE: SERVICE PHOTOGRAPHIQUE

Everywhere in France, towns and villages planted "Liberty Trees" hung with cockades and topped by revolutionary red caps to demonstrate republican zeal. In an allegorical drawing above, a group of sans-culottes dance around a tree set up near the captured Bastille (right) and rout an Austrian army (left) with their patriotic ardour.

queen, was an obvious choice, and the Emperor Leopold had already offered an excuse for taking action. Shortly after the king's flight, he and Frederick William of Prussia had issued the Declaration of Pillnitz, warning France that the Austrians and the Prussians would invade if the other European powers would help. The document was a piece of propaganda, since both monarchs knew no one else had any intention of following their lead. But now the Girondists pretended to take it seriously. In January they issued an ultimatum to the emperor demanding that he renounce the Declaration of Pillnitz and declare his friendship with France.

There was only one possible answer to this insolent demand, but it did not come from Leopold. By an ironic twist of fate, he died on March 1, the day set for his answer. He was succeeded by his son Francis, who was as hot-headed as his father had been cautious.

France prepared for battle, and on April 20, Louis went to the Assembly to make a formal declaration of war against Austria. He spoke in a flat, unemotional tone, and many thought that he was disturbed at the idea of taking action against his wife's native land. In all probability, he was trying to conceal his pleasure at the turn of events.

Louis was now surrounded by Girondists, who had seized control of the government. They had forced the king to dismiss his Feuillant ministers and accept a council of Girondist nominees. It was led by Madame Roland's husband, a balding man twenty years her senior, a lover of red tape, respectable, and weak. Through him she ran the council with an iron hand; she wrote his speeches and memoranda, drafted his letters, and dictated his policy. Madame Roland had finally reached a position of power.

The king detested Roland and his cronies from the beginning. He resented their stuffy, self-righteous airs. During their meetings he read his newspaper, wrote letters, or simply fell asleep in his chair at the head of the table. He interrupted their discussions with funny stories, and whenever he was asked for a decision, he dismissed them and declared the meeting closed. He had accepted them because he could not afford to quarrel with the Girondists in the Assembly, but he had no intention of co-

The royal riding school (below) on the north side of the gardens of the Tuileries became the home of the Assembly. The terms "left" and "right" to describe radicals and conservatives were first used here for the groups that usually sat to the left and right of the president in the centre of the hall. Debates were constantly interrupted by the spectators who crowded the public galleries overlooking the chamber.

operating with them. In fact, as they developed their plans for war, he passed the details to the queen, who sent them to the Austrian ambassador.

The Girondists' plan, drawn up by their only really competent minister, Charles Dumouriez, the minister of foreign affairs, was to strike north into Belgium before the enemy could prepare his defences. But the plan was based on a mistaken idea of the strength of the French army. The Feuillant minister of war, so recently dismissed, had made a tour of inspection and had declared the army ready for action. His report was completely wrong. The French troops were eager and enthusiastic, but that was all. Many of their aristocratic officers had deserted, and the men were undisciplined and ill trained. There was friction between the regular soldiers and the volunteers who had flocked to their country's banner at the urging of the Girondist war-mongers. And the army was short of supplies and ammunition.

Jean Roland was a dull, respectable nonentity who achieved prominence only through the efforts of his shrewish and ambitious wife.

These shortcomings became all too obvious when the columns struck across the Belgian border. At the first sign of the enemy, the French generals ordered a retreat. The common soldiers raised a cry of treason, and one of the generals, Dillon, was caught by his own men and hanged. Leaderless and confused, the troops streamed back into France in rout.

BOTH: MUSEE CARNAVALET, PHOTO BULLOZ

Blame for the disaster lay squarely in the Girondists' laps. They were thunderstruck. Defeat had never entered into their schemes, and they tried to pass the blame onto the king. Their own guilt was hidden under a flurry of emergency measures. They ordered all non-juring priests to leave the country and dismissed the king's royalist bodyguard, replacing it with National Guardsmen. Then they called up twenty thousand *fédérés* from the provinces to guard Paris—or rather, to guard themselves. Louis struck back with a flurry of vetoes: he opposed any attack on the clergy, and he refused to allow the Girondists a bodyguard when they had removed his.

Madame Roland was furious. She felt that the king's attack was directed at her, and she dictated an impertinent letter criticizing Louis' actions which she instructed her husband to read at the next council meeting. Louis knew how to handle insolence: he dismissed Roland and two of his colleagues, and shortly after, Dumouriez resigned before the king's wrath fell on him too. He headed north to take command of the demoralized army, while the empty seats at the council table were filled with Feuillants.

Jeanne Manon Roland, although a fervent patriot, was egotistical, ambitious, and shallow. Like the Girondist leaders who gathered at her dinner parties and fell under her spell, she was idealistic and romantic—fatal virtues in a period that demanded hard-headed and forceful political measures. Her dying words were typical of her: speaking from the scaffold to the clay figure of Liberty that stood nearby, she cried, "O Liberty, what crimes are committed in thy name."

Feelings were running high, and now the sans-culottes took a hand. The forty-eight sections, or wards, of Paris had organized a parade to celebrate the third anniversary of the Tennis Court Oath. As sometimes happened, the parade became a riot. Led by a Cordelier named Antoine Santerre, a popular brewery owner who dispensed free beer to his followers, the crowd of paraders, shouting "Down with the veto" and demanding the recall of the Girondist ministers, invaded the Tuileries. While the queen and her children cowered behind the slim barrier of an overturned table, the king was made to drink the health of the nation and wear a *bonnet rouge*, the red stocking-cap that had recently appeared as the mark of the sans-culottes. But Louis flatly refused to change his mind about the vetoes, and at last the crowd was cleared from the building.

Mayor Pétion, who had replaced Bailly shortly after Lafayette's dismissal, was removed from his post by the Commune for failing to keep order. The Assembly immediately restored him to office; the fault, it said, lay with the king. Lafayette, writing from his headquarters, replied on Louis' behalf, protesting against the riot, and a week later abandoned his post at the front to make a speech to the Assembly. Nobody wanted to listen. The king and queen rejected his offer of protection, and Mayor Pétion would not allow him to address an appeal to his old comrades of the National Guard. Disgusted, the once-popular general returned to his troops with charges of desertion ringing in his ears while the mob burned his effigy at the Palais Royal.

Seven weeks later, when his troops refused to follow him in a march on the Assembly, he deserted and was imprisoned by the Austrians.

The Girondists were in a panic. Their policies had placed them in the hands of the sans-culottes, and they could not rely on the National Guard. To protect themselves, they once more summoned the *fédérés* to Paris, avoiding the king's veto by pretending that the men were to take part in the parade on Bastille Day. But they had lost touch with their own supporters. The National Guardsmen who marched into the city during the hot July of 1792 were even more strongly in favour of a republic than their Parisian cousins. Unlike the respectable tradesmen and businessmen who had founded the National Guard, these *fédérés* were a rough and ready crowd who soon made a bad name for themselves among the more staid citizens of Paris.

The leaders of the sans-culottes, however, gave the *fédérés* a warm welcome. Since their demands for the deposition of the king had been ignored by the Girondists, they had decided to take the law into their own hands, and they needed armed men desperately. Yet they were divided among themselves: half of the sections still backed the Girondists.

Unintentionally, the Girondists themselves gave the quarrelling Parisians a cause to rally around by clearing Lafayette of the charge of desertion that had been raised by his trip to Paris. This drove their Parisian followers over to the insurrectionists; they refused to support a party that seemed to be in league with an enemy of the Revolution.

Pétion was sent to the Assembly with an ultimatum from the citizens of Paris: unless the deputies deposed the king by August 9, the sections would attack the Tuileries and overthrow the monarchy by force. Paralysed by the need for practical measures, the Girondists did nothing while their enemies put the final touches to their plans.

TEXT CONTINUED ON PAGE 86

MUSEE CARNAVALET

Two angry Parisians hang an effigy of the once-popular Lafayette after he deserted his post at the front to protest at the June 20 riot.

For Frenchmen the taking of the Tuileries ranked with the fall of the Bastille. The attackers' banners read

MUSEE DE VERSAILLES

"Liberty, July 14, Equality, August 10". Above, they storm across the corpse-littered courtyard of the palace.

TEXT CONTINUED FROM PAGE 83

All during the ninth an air of uneasiness and expectation hung over the city. Crowds gathered about the palace and drifted aimlessly. In the morning a group led by a red-coated woman on horseback tried to overturn the statue of Louis XIV outside the building, but it was too firmly fixed to its pedestal. At the Assembly over four hundred deputies were absent.

Inside the Tuileries, friends of the king had gathered in droves to defend him. Mandat, the commandant of the National Guard, coolly went about his business of defending the palace. He set up his batteries, posted his men, and mounted guns on the Pont Neuf to keep the sans-culottes of the Cordelier section from joining up with the rest of the crowd. Meanwhile, the attorney general of the Paris department, Roederer, was trying to persuade the king to retreat to the comparative safety of the Assembly.

Under cover of the dark, the insurrectionists began to move. The sections chose new, and illegal, representatives to replace the elected Commune. They ordered Mandat to report to them, but when he reached the city hall, he was murdered, and his body was flung in the river. Santerre the brewer took over command while Pétion sneaked quietly away to the Assembly to save his skin.

In the dawn the alarm bells of Paris began to peal from the city's steeples, and the nondescript army of rebels began their march on the palace. When news of Mandat's death reached Roederer, he realized that the National Guard would desert. He made one last appeal to Louis, and the king, realizing that all hope was gone, at last agreed to leave. Gathering his family together, he led them across the gardens to the riding school.

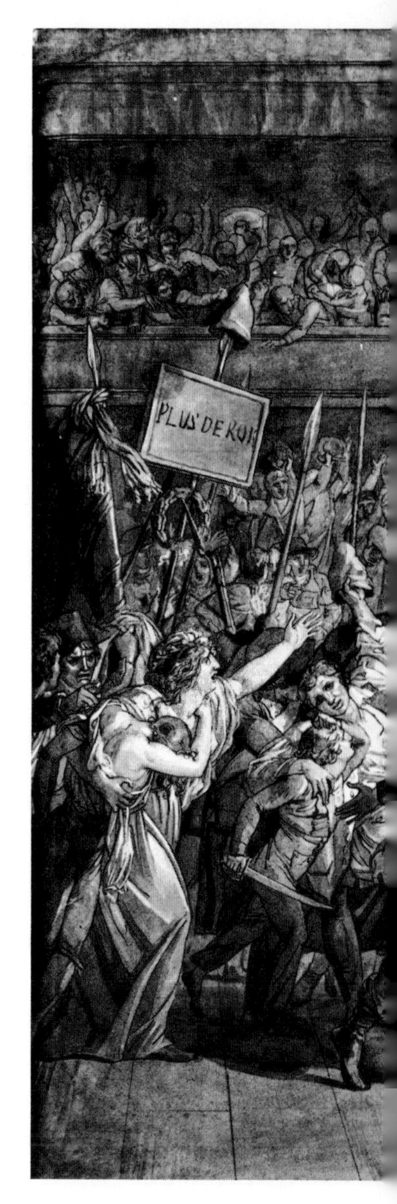

As the party neared the Assembly, it was greeted by a delegation of deputies who invited the king to enter. They disappeared inside the building as the first ominous shots echoed across the garden from the palace behind them.

By ten o'clock a battle was raging around the Tuileries. The National Guard did not resist, but the Swiss Guards were putting up a stiff fight. Delegates of the sections began to pour into the Assembly, claiming that they had been lured into an ambush by the king's men and accusing him of treachery. Louis, who had been lodged with his family in the cramped reporters' box behind the president, was persuaded to order the cease-fire. But no sooner had the defenders laid down their arms than they were overwhelmed by the maddened crowd. A few survived to be flung into prison, but most of them were slaughtered where they

LOUVRE: PHOTO GIRAUDON

Delegates from the sections crowd into the Assembly to ask the king (at right, in the reporters' box) to issue a cease-fire to his Swiss Guards, who have opened fire on the sans-culottes storming the palace.

stood. Their bodies, horribly mutilated, were dragged out of the palace, some even as far as the square in front of the city hall, and left lying on the ground. The mob raged through the Tuileries, smashing windows and hurling furniture through the broken frames in an orgy of destruction.

In the Assembly the deputies solemnly deposed Louis XVI, King of the French, and under pressure from the Commune, ordered the royal family to be imprisoned in the one-time headquarters of the Knights Templar, the grim and gloomy Temple.

V

On the night of January 20, 1793, Louis gathers his family about him in the dining room of the Temple to tell them that he has been condemned to die.

"I DIE INNOCENT"

The night of August 10 changed the whole course of the Revolution. The popular insurrection, which had seized the Commune of Paris and deposed the king, now dominated the Assembly, since no deputy was brave enough, or foolish enough, to oppose it. For the moment the sansculottes had taken over the government of France.

The Parisians quickly showed their strength when the Girondists suggested that the royal family be imprisoned in the Luxembourg Palace. They were promptly overruled, and the Assembly meekly voted to turn the prisoners over to the Commune. So, early in the evening of August 13, 1792, a coach containing Louis, Marie Antoinette, the two children, and their aunt, Madame Élisabeth, rumbled into the courtyard of the Temple. The headquarters of the long-vanished Knights Templar was to be the last residence of the king of the French.

The family was lodged in the main tower of the keep and soon settled into a monotonous routine. They had twenty servants from the Tuileries (although Mayor Pétion later replaced these), good food, and a large library, but their life was far from pleasant. Their jailer, Rocher, sang revolutionary songs at the top of his voice to annoy them, and knowing that Louis detested the smell of tobacco, went out of his way to blow the foul reek of his pipe in the king's face. They were insulted by the prison guards and by the workmen who were building an escape-proof wall round the tower. People in the nearby houses even threw stones at them when they appeared to take their daily walk in the Temple garden. The Commune's agents arrived unannounced at all hours of the day and night to search their rooms, more to annoy them than to search for evidence. But the hardest thing to bear was the constant uncertainty. Few letters reached the royal family without being censored, and newspapers were forbidden. None of them could guess what was to be their fate.

The Assembly had not yet faced that problem. The deputies had an even more urgent question to consider: how

France was to be governed, since the charter of 1791 was clearly meaningless in August, 1792. It was finally decided to call for fresh elections; a new Assembly would be needed to tackle the problem of drawing up a new code of government. (The new body was to be called the Convention, after the Convention of Philadelphia, which two decades before had drawn up a democratic constitution for the United States.) In the meantime, the deputies selected a temporary executive council of six ministers to replace the king. Five of them were Girondists, led by Roland in his old post of minister of the interior. The sixth was a most unlikely teammate for the idealistic Girondists—Georges Jacques Danton, the tough and decisive boss of the Cordeliers.

MUSEE CARNAVALET: PHOTO BULLOZ

In this eyewitness sketch, Louis (third from right) leads his family for a stroll in the garden of their prison. The tower in which they lived looms in the background.

Danton became minister of justice, and since he had been elected by a greater majority than any of his colleagues, he assumed leadership of the Executive Council. Even without the Assembly's backing, he would have dominated it by sheer force of personality.

Danton was a big man in size as well as in spirit. His huge frame, with its brutally battered prize-fighter's face, towered above his colleagues in any gathering. A contemporary had called him the Lord High Sans-culotte, and the title fitted him perfectly, for he was, in some ways, no better than some of his shady friends—many of whom were outright criminals. He himself had been accused of taking bribes from Mirabeau and the king, and he certainly spent more money than his salary as a deputy could cover.

Despite his toughness, Danton's personal background was as respectable as any Girondist could wish: his father was a prominent lawyer in the little town of Arcis, eighty-five miles south-east of Paris. Danton himself had studied law and was a man of wide culture, well-read, fluent in English and Italian, and like the Girondists, a classical scholar. Unlike the Girondists, however, he had become a convinced democrat during his student days in Paris, for his sympathies were always with the underdog. There was a story that he had once been seen treading water in the Seine, where he often swam for exercise, shaking his fist and howling curses at the Bastille. The story is typical of the man, for his feelings were passionate and forthright; he never shrank from the use of force if he felt it was necessary. Only his marriage tamed him a little, for he was devoted to his gentle wife.

Danton was a popular man, and a man of the people. He had founded the Cordeliers to give the sans-culottes of Paris a voice, and the people idolized him for it. Although

MUSEE CARNAVALET

Danton, while one of the most admirable figures of the Revolution, was certainly among the ugliest. Three violent childhood accidents had left their mark on a face that was also ravaged with the scars of smallpox. Yet Danton overcame his physical handicaps by his dedication to the cause of the Revolution and by his flaming eloquence.

he antagonized many of his fellow politicians, many more respected him for his quick intelligence, his conviction, and his fiery eloquence.

Being a realistic politician, Danton was prepared to co-operate with the Girondists in the interest of a united, free, and democratic France. He might have been able to bridge the gap between them and the sans-culottes of Paris, but the growing rivalry between the provinces and Paris gradually put any hope of a peaceful compromise out of the question. Neither the Girondists, who inclined towards the provincial point of view, nor the Parisians would yield an inch, and each side was determined to destroy the other. The Girondists hoped that the elections would throw out the insurrectionists; the sans-culottes retaliated by forcing the Assembly to pass a series of reforms that were far more democratic than anything the Girondists had contemplated. The vote was extended to every Frenchman over the age of twenty-one; army commissions were thrown open to all on the basis of merit; and compensation to landlords for their lost feudal dues was abolished.

The Commune's police powers were also widened: it was given the authority to arrest suspected counter-revolutionaries and to make house-to-house searches without a warrant. And finally, the National Guard was put under the control of the Paris sections, adding teeth to the threat of popular violence. If it came to outright war between the Assembly and Paris, the city now had a well-trained fighting force at its command.

The Girondists' cause received a rude shock when the war they had fostered took an alarming turn for the worse. At the end of August an army of Prussian, Austrian, and *émigré* troops, under the Duke of Brunswick, moved across the border and began a cautious march on Paris. The border town of Longwy fell on August 23. A week later, the fortress of Verdun was surrendered by its royalist garrison, and the revolutionary commandant of the town blew out his brains in despair. Only Dumouriez' untried army stood between Brunswick and his goal (see map on page 95).

One of the victims of the mob that invaded the Carmes prison during the massacres of September, 1792, was Afry, the aged commander of the Swiss Guards (under 1, above).

Danton rose to the occasion superbly. He had been against the war from the start, but now, when his country was in danger, he roused the people in a voice that no one could resist. "The bells you hear," he cried to his fellow citizens, "are not an alarm but the signal of an awakening. We must be daring, and still more daring, and daring yet again, and France will be saved!" The men of Paris listened and responded. Within days thousands of volunteers were streaming out of the city to join the fight.

As the city was stripped of its young men a wave of fear swept through the people. Prompted by the newspapers, a wild rumour spread that the aristocrats and priests in the city jails were planning to break out and massacre the citizens of Paris. The Cordelier leader Jean Paul Marat and other rabble-rousing journalists fanned the flames of hatred and panic and screamed for the blood of the conspirators. In an atmosphere of hysteria, no one paused to wonder how a handful of jailed "conspirators", less than four hundred in number, could overcome a city of half a million.

Marat was foremost among the political writers in rousing popular feeling. Through the columns of his newspaper, *The People's Friend*, he had built up a reputation as the champion of the people by his constant attacks on the authorities. But, in a sense, Marat had no politics; he was simply against anyone who held power, and it made no difference to him whether they were the ministers, the aristocrats, the royalists, the Girondists, or the courts. He flailed at them all without fear or favour.

Yet Marat was not a typical sans-culotte. He had studied medicine and had travelled abroad. In England, he had moved in the best circles and had been awarded an honorary medical degree by a leading university. On his return to France, he had been appointed surgeon to the Duke of Orléans' bodyguard and had a large and prosperous practice among the duke's friends.

Even so, Marat was a deeply discontented man. He craved recognition as a scientist and thinker, but his odd and often ridiculous theories were derided by established scholars, and the French Academy of Science rejected his application for membership. His ventures into the field of philosophy were subjected to a withering attack by no less a figure than Voltaire. Frustration and bitterness began to twist Marat's mind. He became convinced that there was a conspiracy among recognized scholars to rob him of fame and glory. Strange illnesses began to plague him. He suf-

The Abbaye prison was a scene of frightful carnage during the massacres. Below at left, one of the captives recoils in horror at the sight of the corpses littering the yard as the leader of the killers (at centre) gestures his condemnation. Meanwhile, at right, the butchery continues without pause.

MUSEE CARNAVALET: PHOTO GIRAUDON

In his masterpiece, "Roll Call of the Last Victims", Charles Louis Muller depicted a typical prison scene during the Revolution, with an official (standing to the left of the doorway) reading out a list of the condemned. The man in the chair at centre is the poet André Chénier, who was executed in 1794. Over 1,100 prisoners died in the massacres that were inspired by the bloodthirsty sans-culotte journalist Jean Paul Marat (opposite)

fered from blinding headaches and crippling leg pains for which there was no medical explanation.

The Revolution gave him a chance to revenge himself on those who enjoyed the power and prestige that had been denied to him. His attacks on authority became increasingly violent, and he had to go into hiding several times to avoid arrest. After accusing the king of planning the massacre of the Champ de Mars, he took refuge for weeks in the sewers and dark corners of Paris.

Always an ugly little man, he emerged from this experience a nightmare figure. His yellowed skin was covered with the vile sores of the disease that was to affect him for the rest of his life; his eyes rolled, and his limbs twitched uncontrollably. No less appalling than his twitches and the lank hair that hung into his eyes were the greasy rags in which he habitually dressed. Even his friends kept their distance. Yet, despite his appearance, Marat's sinister influence was wider than ever. He seemed to be in the thick of every disturbance in the city, and his name was linked with the dreadful events that followed the departure of Danton's volunteers for the front.

He was appointed to the Paris Watch Committe, which controlled the police and the prisons. On September 2, he was carried in triumph to a meeting of the committee in the mayor's residence by a mob of supporters, among whom were the ragged, drunken Marseillais, the rowdiest and most lawless of the *fédérés*.

Later that same day, several coaches loaded with non-juring priests left the mayor's house, bound for the Abbaye prison across the river. Outside the Abbaye, they were halted by a mob, many of them the same Marseilles *fédérés* who had followed Marat earlier. They dragged the priests from the coaches and butchered them in the street. Leaving the bodies lying in the gutter, the mob moved to the nearby Carmes prison. They broke into the building and began to murder the 150 priests imprisoned there. At the height of the massacre at Carmes, Maillard, the hero of the Bastille, arrived with the Commune's order that the prisoners were to be questioned before being killed. Sitting behind a table in the corridor outside the cells, his wire-rimmed glasses perched on his thin nose, this mock judge presided over a series of mock trials before turning the terrified victims over to the butchers. Not one was acquitted.

MUSEE CARNAVALET: PHOTO GIRAUDON

The Revolution's new armies were hardened in a series of engagements along France's northern border in the areas shown on the map below.

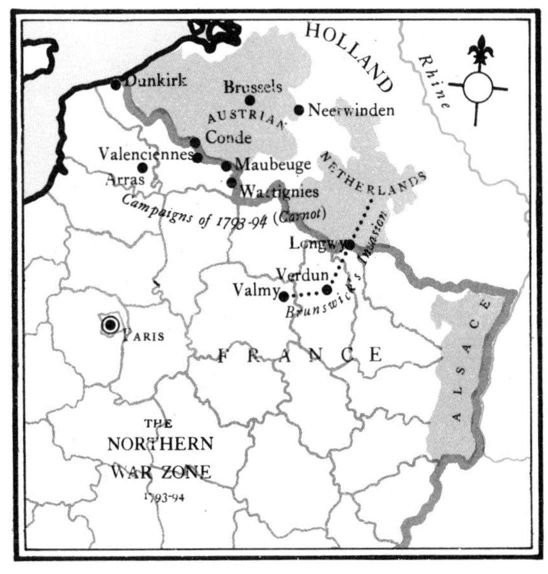

When they had finished their bloody work at the Carmes, the mob surged back to the Abbaye prison, accompanied by the conscientious Maillard. Night had fallen, and before long, two bonfires were blazing in the courtyard of the prison to light the slaughter. Three hundred more wretches were added to the mounting toll, and their hacked and headless bodies were piled into a ghastly mound while the gutters ran red.

Two other prisons, the Conciergerie, attached to the Palace of Justice, and the Châtelet, were invaded by mobs on that dreadful night. The following day, the same horrible scenes were repeated at the prison of La Force.

The killings had turned into a mindless orgy of bloodshed as normally respectable citizens joined in the massacres. In five days, eleven hundred victims fell to the fury of the mob. Yet less than thirty of the dead were aristocrats, and less than three hundred were priests. Much of the savagery had been spent on common criminals, women, beggars, and children. The men who might have halted the massacres—Robespierre, Danton, Mayor Pétion, Santerre, the commander of the National Guard, Roland, the minister of the interior—did nothing. Some of them approved of the killings, and Roland called them "a sort of justice".

Whether any of these men actually helped to plan the massacres is not known. Even Marat's part is shrouded in darkness, and his motives are unclear. If he was hoping to terrify the Paris electors into voting for sans-culotte candidates, he succeeded; he himself was among them. If he was hoping to scare the whole of France, he failed; in a reaction against Paris, the provincial voters returned the Girondists to power in the Convention.

The deputies of the Convention differed in one important respect from those of the previous assemblies. Where formerly there had been many small power groups gathered around leading figures, there were now two distinct parties, one to the right and one to the left of the uncommitted Centre.

To the right were the Girondists, who now appeared as the champions of the provinces and the upper middle-class men of property. Their policy was to make France a federation of self-governing districts by building up the power of the departments. In opposition to them stood the Mountain, the democrats who had taken over the Jacobin Club after the Feuillants and the Girondists had deserted. They drew their strength from the Commune and the sans-culottes, and their point of view was Parisian. The Moun-

ARCHIVES NATIONALES: PHOTO JOSSE-LALANCE

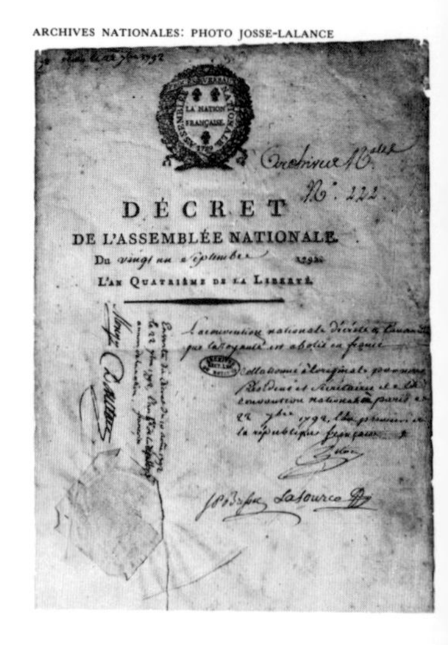
LA NATION FRANÇAISE

DÉCRET
DE L'ASSEMBLÉE NATIONALE.
L'An Quatrième de la Liberté.

tain wanted a strong central government based on Paris, and their cause was served by the strongest men in the Convention—Robespierre, Danton, and the followers of Marat and Hébert, who were known as the *enragés*, or "maniacs".

However, for the moment the Girondists held the upper hand; the voters had returned them to power, and fortune smiled on them. On the first day of the new session, Dumouriez, their general, won a victory, which turned the tide of the war.

Dumouriez had been unwilling to face Brunswick in open battle. His troops were green, and he remembered

On September 21, 1792, the Assembly issued a decree (opposite) that abolished the monarchy, but the deputies refused to declare France a republic. However, the event was greeted by joyful displays such as a mock funeral of the monarchy, below, which took place in the city of Strasbourg.

BIBLIOTHEQUE NATIONALE: PHOTO GIRAUDON

only too well the early disasters of France's volunteer army. So he resorted to defensive manoeuvring. Slipping around the advancing Prussians, he took up a position near Valmy, not far from Verdun. Brunswick was forced to turn and defend his badly stretched supply lines. However, he was confident that he could wipe out the French with ease, since the armies were roughly equal in numbers, and his was better trained. But he had reckoned without two things: the fighting spirit of Dumouriez' volunteers and the superb French artillery, which was a legacy of far-sighted generals of the Old Régime.

BIBLIOTHEQUE NATIONALE: SERVICE PHOTOGRAPHIQUE

The French victory at Valmy, although it failed to smash the Austrians, still forced Brunswick to retreat. Above, one of his tired, tattered soldiers heads for home.

The French troops were entrenched along a ridge on which stood the windmill of Valmy. Brunswick sent in his Prussians to sweep the French from the slope in a head-on assault, but the attack bogged down in the mud. Most of the Prussians remained pinned by deadly cannonades for the rest of the day, while the few who reached the top of the ridge were flung back by the cheering volunteers.

There were few casualties on that day, but Dumouriez' victory spelled the end of Brunswick's plans. Slowly, cautiously, he led his men back to the border along roads that were rivers of mud under the weeping autumn skies. Dumouriez had saved the city, the nation, and the Girondists, and was rewarded with supreme command of the French armies. Within six weeks he had led them on a campaign of conquest that placed most of Belgium and a part of the Rhine Province under French control.

The Girondists were not slow to take advantage of his success. On the afternoon of September 21, the day after Valmy, the Convention formally abolished the monarchy, and on the following day decreed that all public documents should be headed "The First Year of the French Republic". Three weeks later, the Girondists set up a committee, packed with their own men, to draw up a new constitution —a Girondist constitution—for the new-born republic. Then they turned on their enemies.

They might have been able to swing the Centre over to their side, but they offended many deputies by spiteful personal attacks on the leaders of the Mountain. Roland led the assault by flailing at the Commune. He accused it of breeding disorder, hampering the ministers, fixing the elections—all of which was true—but he spoiled his case through over-eagerness. His charges became more and more ridiculous as he seized on every rumour to discredit the Parisians. In the end, he irritated even his own friends.

Robespierre defended the sans-culottes against Roland's

charges, and he too came under fire. A leading Girondist named Louvet, who was a pretentious and unsuccessful novelist and a great favourite of Madame Roland's, denounced Robespierre and accused him of wanting to be a dictator. The Jacobin leader had little trouble defending himself against such a flimsy charge, and he succeeded in making Louvet look a fool. In October, disillusioned with the Girondists, Danton resigned from the Executive Council. He began to ally himself with Robespierre, and his replacement on the council, who had been a Girondist, immediately followed suit. Shortly afterward, Georges Couthon, an influential deputy of the Centre and a prominent member of the constitutional committee, joined the growing list of defectors to the Mountain. The Girondist axe was proving to be a double-edged weapon.

The Mountain was growing in strength day by day, and its clamour for the king's condemnation, which had been ignored at the beginning of the session, became louder and more insistent. At last, while the Girondists faltered, events played into their opponents' hands.

On November 20, Roland, acting on information given to him by a disgruntled locksmith named Gamain, discovered an iron chest in the royal apartments at the Tuileries. Gamain had made the chest for the king in May, and when it was opened, it was found to contain all the evidence that was needed to convict the king. It was crammed with his secret papers, including Mirabeau's notes, the plans for the flight to Varennes, and details concerning the money that the king had sent to the *émigrés*.

On December 11, the king was brought before the Convention to be tried. For three hours, he sat in his olive-coloured silk coat and answered his accusers without flinching. But his answers were clumsy lies. He denied any knowledge of the iron chest. He claimed to have "forgotten" about Mirabeau's notes. He said that documents written in his own hand were forgeries. He sat impassive while a long indictment containing thirty-three counts was read to him. Only the final accusation, "You have caused the blood of Frenchmen to be spilled", brought any reaction. At these cutting words, he heaved himself to his feet, crying, "No, sir! I have never shed the blood of Frenchmen." And as they led him away, the tears were coursing down his face.

The king's defence was presented on December 26. He had been allowed to choose his own defence lawyers, but there were few willing to serve. At last, Malesherbes, a retired attorney over seventy years of age, and a courageous

BIBLIOTHEQUE NATIONALE: PHOTO GIRAUDON

Roland, seated at left, raises his hands in horror as the door of the "iron chest" swings open to reveal Mirabeau as the skeleton in the royal closet. Mirabeau's notes were included in the incriminating documents concealed in the chest.

young lawyer named Sèze offered to defend him. They were given only ten days to examine the unsorted mess of documents from the iron chest, but they knew that they could not win by trying to deny the charges anyway. They pinned their hopes on the argument that the Convention could not try the king at all, since it was not a recognized judicial body. They failed; the Mountain was determined to offer the king as a sacrifice to the Revolution.

The debate on the king's fate lasted twenty-four days. The Girondists, still trying to find a compromise, proposed that the verdict be decided by a vote of the whole nation. The Jacobins, who saw the king slipping through their fingers if this happened, opposed the motion. They argued that the people had entrusted the Convention with the decision by

While Abbé Edgeworth stands in prayer beside the body of his dead master, the executioner displays Louis' severed head to the crowd.

electing it. Happily for them, the proposal was defeated.

At last, in a stormy session that lasted for four days, the deputies cast their votes. By an overwhelming majority, they found Louis guilty; by a hair's breadth, they condemned him to death.

Louis received the news calmly on January 20. He asked for three days to prepare his soul to meet its Maker, but this the Convention refused. It did, however, allow him to send for a non-juring Irish priest who had been the queen's confessor, the Abbé Edgeworth.

That same night the king saw his family for the last time. They met in the dining-room of the Temple. With his son standing between his knees, the women in a grief-stricken circle about him, Louis gently told them that he was to die. His son asked bravely if he could go with his father to the scaffold to ask the people for pardon; the women wept. Then they parted, the king promising to see them again the following morning. But he never saw them again; he broke his promise to spare them the pain of a second farewell.

BIBLIOTHEQUE NATIONALE: SERVICE PHOTOGRAPHIQUE

Later that night, he made his final confession to the Irish priest and slept soundly. On the morning of the day of his execution, he heard mass in his room, the altar a bureau which Clery, his valet, had dragged out from the wall. He seemed at peace with himself and even found time to commiserate with Clery, who had spent the night in an armchair. He gave the man an envelope containing locks of his hair for the family. Then he braced himself to meet his executioners.

At nine, Santerre arrived with the escort. Louis shook hands with his faithful servant, and turning, marched out between his guards with a firm step. A few minutes later, a roar of drums and a clamour of trumpets told Clery that his master had set out on his last ride.

At the foot of the scaffold, ringed about with drummers beating an ominous roll, the executioner shaved the king's neck for the blade. Louis mounted the steps unaided and moved to the edge of the platform. At his gesture, the drumsticks were stilled, the drumbeats echoed into silence, the crowd grew still. "My people, I die innocent. . ." he began, but at an angry wave from Santerre, the drummers sprang to life again, and the rest of the words were drowned in their thunder. In an instant, the king had been tied down to the guillotine. The steel blade fell. The king was dead.

A moment later, the executioner held up the bloody head for all to see. But there was no one to say the traditional words on the death of a king. Now the people had a new litany: "The king is dead; long live the republic!"

VI

TRIUMPH OF THE JACOBINS

The bells that pealed out the execution of the last of the Bourbons tolled the death knell of the Girondists. They had been kept in power by a series of lucky accidents; now their luck deserted them. Disasters piled up thick and fast, and the Girondists were unable to cope with them.

The first hint of trouble appeared after the king's trial, which strained the group severely. Most of the Girondist leaders had voted for immediate execution, but the majority of the rank and file wanted a lesser penalty. The deputies of the Mountain, waiting like hungry wolves, closed in for the kill. The death of Louis made their task even simpler than they had anticipated.

Outside France, the event drove the English into an alliance with the Austrians and the Prussians. The English remembered the Girondists' boast that the French army would carry republicanism to every nation in Europe; they had seen that boast carried out in Belgium, after Dumouriez' invasion. Besides, the French advance northward threatened their Dutch allies, and if Holland fell, France would have the ports she needed to challenge England's control of the seas. In January, a nervous British government seized several ships that were about to sail for France with badly needed cargoes of grain, and then ordered its fleet to prepare for action.

The Girondist leader Brissot was forced to declare war on England before the English declared war on France. He tried to make the best of a hopeless situation by delivering another "crusade" speech, but nothing could hide the fact that France was now ringed with enemies.

It was typical of the Girondists that they chose this

The medal opposite commemorates the Jacobins, who challenged the government leadership in 1793. Another threat to stability was foreign arms; the English especially were shocked by the execution of Louis (cartoon above).

MUSEE CARNAVALET

desperate moment to quarrel with the one man who could have saved them, General Dumouriez. Dumouriez had grown steadily more disillusioned with the Girondists as they added blunder to stupid blunder. Desperate for money, since they had never faced up to France's financial problems, the Girondists had hoped to make the army pay for its keep, despite Dumouriez' pledge to the Belgians that he came as a liberator, not as a conqueror. They had made his position in Belgium impossible by a decree in mid-December, 1792, which ordered the French army to confiscate the treasure of the Belgian churches. A pack of commissioners was sent to Belgium to see that the decree was carried out. They were all deputies of the Mountain, carefully selected by the Girondists to reduce the number of Jacobin votes in the Convention. But the move was a boomerang. The commissioners roused the Belgians to the point of revolt by stripping the churches of their priceless works of art and by destroying those that could not be removed. At the same time, by spreading Jacobin propaganda among the troops, the commissioners succeeded in turning Dumouriez' own men against him.

The Girondists' military leader, General Charles Dumouriez, is shown here surveying battle plans.

Late in 1792, when the Girondists ordered Dumouriez to invade Holland, he refused. He pointed out that it would be suicide to make any move that left his rear exposed to the angry Belgians. He also complained that his troops had no supplies or ammunition. Upon investigation of this charge, it was discovered that the Girondist war minister, Pache, had gone over to the Mountain, and that on Marat's orders, he was turning over arms and ammunition to the Paris sections. "The patriots at home," he explained, "needed weapons too."

For Dumouriez, this was the last straw. Disgusted alike with the Girondists and with the Mountain, whose petty quarrels threatened the safety of the nation, he decided to overthrow the Convention and seize power for himself. While he was perfecting his plans the Girondist defences were dealt another shattering blow.

To prepare for the monumental struggle facing France in the spring of 1793, the Girondists had ordered the recruitment of 300,000 fresh troops. In March, enrolment began in the Vendée department on the Atlantic coast at the mouth of the Loire. The interior of the Vendée was one of the poorest areas in France, a region of rocky hills and bad soil. The people were backward, poverty-stricken, and fiercely religious. They had protected their non-juring priests from arrest and they had remained loyal to the

BIBLIOTHEQUE NATIONALE: PHOTO BULLOZ

This contemporary engraving illustrates an early episode of the wars of the Vendée: the rebels defend a bridge against government forces by blocking it with a manure cart. The royalist Vendeans had on their side in the war good hunting guns and keen knowledge of the terrain.

monarchy; they wanted no part of the Revolution. Yet they were being asked to fight for the republic by the men who had outlawed their priests and put the king to death.

Enraged by fiery sermons from the clergy, the Vendeans rose in revolt. Small bands of peasants, armed at first only with farm tools, defeated the National Guard detachments sent out to deal with them. Soon the aristocrats of the Vendée, many of them as poor as their own peasants, joined the movement and began to train the rebels in the art of guerrilla warfare. In an incredibly short time they had organized an efficient army of irregulars completely familiar with the rough and rugged terrain from which they were able to defy the National Guard with ease. In lightning raids the rebels cut to pieces the garrisons of several towns, raided supply dumps, cut lines of communication, and then retreated to the safety of their isolated farms and villages, from which they thumbed their noses at the government troops. Before long, the counter-revolution spread into other districts, many of which were still royalist, and the Girondists were faced with a menace from within almost as dangerous as the threat from without.

And on the same day that saw the opening of the long-dreaded counter-revolution, an Austrian army led by the Duke of Coburg smashed Dumouriez' troops at Neerwinden, just east of Brussels. Dumouriez attacked his superiors, bitterly complaining that their plunder of the Belgian churches and their general incompetence had led

to his defeat. The Girondists reacted by sending a commission to his headquarters to arrest him, but he was too quick for them. The defiant general made the commissioners prisoners and turned them over to the Austrians as hostages for the prisoners in the Temple; he had decided to put his long-prepared plan into action. Making a truce with the Austrians to protect his back, he called on the army to follow him to Paris. His appeal fell on deaf ears; the Jacobin propagandists had done their work well, and the men mutinied against his orders. So, on April 4, 1793, disgusted with the whole Revolution, General Dumouriez took horse and deserted to the Austrian lines.

The Girondists had stumbled into a hopeless situation. Enemy forces stood poised on the borders of France, and the French army was dispirited and short of supplies. The leading French general had deserted. The ports were blockaded by the British fleet. The Vendée and Brittany were in revolt, and food supplies, always short, were nearing famine level. The treasury was empty, and the assignats were steadily falling in value. Within the Convention the Mountain grew in strength day by day, and by the beginning of 1793, its constant battering was crumbling the Girondist defences.

The assault was led by Danton and Marat. Danton rallied the people once again with a rousing speech, claiming that the war must be carried on until the French nation extended to its "natural borders": the Rhine, the Atlantic, the Pyrenees, and the Alps. This—in contrast to Brissot's high-flown idea of a crusade—was a down-to-earth appeal that every Frenchman could understand. Marat's contribution was a new series of disturbances intended to terrify the Convention. At the beginning of February, 1793, the Cordeliers, the *fédérés*, and the sections published manifestoes calling for an end to the Girondist rule. Food riots provoked by the sans-culottes left a trail of broken and looted shops throughout Paris. And on February 8, a new insurrectionary Commune was set up that led the sections in a march on the Convention. Its intention was to throw out the Girondists who had failed to vote for the king's execution. However, Santerre's National Guard turned the marchers back, and they had to be content with wrecking

The gentleman opposite bravely wears the uniform of a delegate on mission to the army. Yet magnificent republican uniforms were sometimes seen in retreat—note the detail above from a view of the Battle of Neerwinden.

the Girondist newspaper offices and smashing their printing presses. Finally Marat issued a circular to the Jacobin clubs, calling openly for the destruction of the Girondists. "Friends, we have been betrayed," it read. "The foul treason of our enemies has at last achieved its goal, and their collaborator Dumouriez is marching on Paris. To arms, republicans . . ."

In an atmosphere of chaos, denunciation, and terror, the Mountain was able to swing the wavering Centre to its side. It forced through a series of emergency measures that wrested power from the local governing bodies and concentrated it in Paris, where the Mountain held control. Even the Girondists had seen the need for stronger measures in the crisis that faced France, but it was the Mountain that now proposed them, and it was the Mountain that took the credit for them.

On the day after Neerwinden, Danton suggested that a special court was needed to handle crimes against the state, and the Revolutionary Tribunal was voted into being. Its members—judges, prosecutors, and jury alike—were appointed by the Convention, not freely elected. Its jurymen were obliged to vote openly, and no appeals were allowed from the Tribunal's decisions. It had authority to try "all counter-revolutionary acts, all attacks upon the Republic and the security of the state, and all plots hostile to the liberty, equality, and sovereign rights of the people". In a short time the Revolutionary Tribunal had become a tool of the Mountain; the public prosecutor, Fouquier-Tinville, was a distant relation of Camille Desmoulins, and the members of the jury were all Paris sans-culottes.

The strength of the sans-culottes, who supported the Mountain, was also increased. In March, the watch committees, which they dominated, were authorized to seek out and expel suspicious foreigners in their sections and to issue passports to every loyal citizen. Soon after, all *émigrés* were declared legally dead, and their property was confiscated by the nation. Finally, on April 6, the Mountain took a momentous step by creating the Committee of Public Safety.

The new agency inherited some of the powers of its predecessor, the Girondists' General Defence Committee, which had been founded earlier in the year as a link between the ministers and the Convention. But the earlier committee had been inefficient, as were most Girondist creations: it had been too large, and it had held its sessions in public. The Mountain needed something more powerful

BIBLIOTHEQUE NATIONALE: SERVICE PHOTOGRAPHIQUE

and less open to inspection and criticism, so it gained control of the older committee by the election of Robespierre, Danton, and Desmoulins—and then destroyed it.

The Committee of Public Safety was streamlined, powerful, and ruthlessly efficient. And, from the beginning, it was in the hands of the Mountain; Danton was its first leader. Its nine members held their meetings in secret, and they had control of large secret funds to pay for the services of spies and informers. Officially, the new committee, like the old General Defence Committee, was supposed to serve as a link between the deputies and the Executive Council, but its members lost no time in using their new emergency powers to replace the ministers. After all, they were supposed to protect the public safety, which was threatened both by foreign invaders and by traitors, who flourished on every side.

As food became scarcer during the Revolution, and as the value of the new paper money became less, more and more assignats were needed to buy bread. Troops were dispatched to some critical areas to distribute food money. In this painting (which may have been done as political propaganda) officers hand out bags of money to eager peasants.

BIBLIOTHEQUE NATIONALE: SERVICE PHOTOGRAPHIQUE

In this romantic painting, troops and citizens led to the Convention by François Hanriot on May 31, 1793, are requested to disperse from before the Tuileries Palace.

The Girondists, unable to halt the momentum of the movement on the floor of the Convention, redoubled their attacks on the leaders of the Mountain. Their choice of targets was limited. Danton and Robespierre both enjoyed great popularity and prestige; it would be suicidal to pick on them. Marat, however, had left them an opening with his bloodthirsty circular to the Jacobin clubs. He seemed to be a perfect victim, since many of the deputies of the Centre also hated him enough to vote for his impeachment. But the Girondists had not reckoned with the new strength of the Mountain. On April 15, five days before Marat's trial, the Convention was besieged by the crowd from the sections demanding that the leading Girondists be expelled from the assembly. Turned away by the Girondist president, the crowd reappeared five days later and was rebuffed a second time. When Marat appeared before his Jacobin friends of the Revolutionary Tribunal on April 23, he was cleared of the charges amid scenes of wild enthusiasm. A crowd carried him in triumph from the courtroom to the Convention and then to the Jacobin Club. The Girondists seemed incapable of learning from their mistakes. Marat's release merely urged them on to further follies.

They denounced the Commune again and again, appealing to the deputies to crush it out of existence and to move the Convention away from Paris. They called for help from the provinces. They loudly supported the establishment of a Commission of Twelve to investigate the activities of the sans-culottes and to bring their ringleaders to justice. As a result, Hébert and several of his colleagues were arrested and imprisoned.

On the last day of May, the sections organized to defend themselves against the Girondists. They set up their own Committee of Public Safety and prepared for a fight to the death. The National Guard was mobilized under its new commander, François Hanriot, a rowdy, drunken ex-clerk who had once worked for the customs department. (Santerre had been dismissed for defending the Convention in March.) Hanriot moved swiftly. He closed the gates of Paris and rounded up the most important Girondist sympathizers in the city, including Madame Roland. Only her husband slipped through his fingers; the rest were flung into prison. All the following day, Hanriot was busy moving his men and guns into strategic positions around the Tuileries Palace, which had become the new home of the Convention just three weeks before.

François Hanriot

Here, in a stormy session that threatened to turn into a riot, the Mountain was preparing the finishing stroke for its enemies. The deputies of the Mountain forced through a motion that abolished the Commission of Twelve, and they released the imprisoned members of the Commune.

Early the next morning, June 2, 1793, representatives from the Commune repeated its demand for the arrest of the Girondist leaders. Once again they were turned out by the president, but a hand-picked audience in the galleries took up the cry. Amid the uproar, the frightened legislators voted to close the session and then tried to leave the palace. They got no farther than the doors. Outside, they found ranks of blue-coated National Guardsmen, muskets at the ready, backed by a huge, hostile crowd.

Marat had darted outside through a side exit and was beseeching the soldiers to stand firm. Under the spell of his fiery words, the crowd began to chant "Clean out the Convention" at the deputies who were milling about in confusion. Dazed by the tumult, they turned back into the hall

TEXT CONTINUED ON PAGE 114

Having been cleared by the Revolutionary Tribunal, Marat is hailed by the populace of the Paris sections. In this pai

MUSEE LAMBINET, VERSAILLES: PHOTO GIRAUDON

g by Boilly, Marat (with bandaged head) is carried by the crowd beneath the soaring arches of the Palace of Justice.

BOTH: MUSEE LAMBINET, VERSAILLES: PHOTO JOSSE-LALANCE

Charlotte Corday, as seen in the portrait at right by Hauer, was a comely and moody girl. Her arrival at Marat's door is pictured in the drawing above.

TEXT CONTINUED FROM PAGE 111

and took their seats. When they were all in place, Marat read off a list of the twenty-nine Girondists who were to be arrested, and on Couthon's motion, the marked men were formally dismissed from the Convention and led away through the booing sans-culottes to be imprisoned in their homes.

All of them knew that their days were numbered, and at the end of June, several of them, following Roland's example, escaped from Paris in disguise. They headed for Caen, in Normandy, the nearest place of safety.

One of their most fervent disciples lived in Caen. She was a handsome young countrywoman, the daughter of a poor but aristocratic family, named Charlotte Corday. Like the Girondists she admired, her head was stuffed with the works of Rousseau and the classical writers. However, she added to her romantic dreams of glory the hard-headed practicality of the Norman farmers. For months before the arrival of the fugitive deputies, she had been tortured by her inability to help their cause. The expulsion of her heroes from the Convention decided her; she would strike a blow against the sans-culotte traitors that would not be forgotten.

She selected Marat as her target, as the Girondists had already done to their cost. For Charlotte, he represented the worst of the Jacobin movement, and she planned a theatrical assassination on the floor of the Convention. Marat was to die at her hands as Caesar had died at Brutus'.

Her plans for a spectacular scene were foiled from the start. On her arrival in Paris, late in the afternoon of July 11, she discovered that Marat, now almost completely disabled by disease, no longer took his seat in the convention hall. He remained at home, immersed in a bath of mineral salts to soothe his pain. But the determined girl was not to be turned aside by trifles. Marat had to die.

On the morning of July 13, she was up and about early, as was her country-bred habit. She dressed carefully and pinned in the bodice of her dress an "Address to the French People", which explained her motives in the rather high-flown terms that the Girondists loved. More practically, she added her birth certificate, so that no one would have any doubts about her name. Then she bought a kitchen knife with a six-inch steel blade and set out for Marat's lodgings, in the same street as the Cordeliers Club.

PERMISSION OF THE TRUSTEES OF THE BRITISH MUSEUM

Throughout Europe there was sympathy for the cause of Charlotte Corday. To many, Marat and the leaders of the Revolution seemed tyrants far worse than kings. The artist of this English cartoon neglected to show Marat in the tub at the time of Charlotte's visit.

MUSEE DE VERSAILLES: ARCHIVES PHOTOGRAPHIQUES

Planned as a public memorial to the martyr, David's "Death of Marat" is nonetheless stark and unsentimental. In his left hand, he holds Charlotte's original letter; in his right is a pen to add the names of the Girondists.

Here she was turned away by Marat's jealous common-law wife, Simonne Evrard, who refused to let her in. Charlotte returned to her hotel and wrote a note to Marat explaining that she had information concerning Girondists in Caen and asking for an interview. By evening, she had received no reply, so she retraced her steps to Marat's house. This time, she found the doors unguarded and a scene of bustle and confusion in the outer rooms where Marat's newspaper was being prepared. She had almost reached the inner room, where Marat was sitting in his bath, before Simonne noticed her.

Inside, Marat heard the sound of raised voices and ordered Charlotte to enter. She was shocked at the sight of the "monster" she had come so far to kill. His ravaged, wrinkled body was propped up in his tub, his head was swathed in vinegar-soaked rags. Before him, resting on the sides of the bath, was a plank that served as his desk.

He motioned her, courteously enough, to a stool beside him and asked her business. She reminded him of the note she had sent earlier and offered to give him first-hand information about the rising that was being planned. She listed for him the names of the Girondists who had taken refuge in Caen. Busily, he scratched them down with his quill on a sheet of paper. When she had finished, he looked up and said with an evil grin, "They will soon be guillotined."

At his words, Charlotte snatched the knife from her bodice and plunged it into his chest. Then turning calmly, she walked out of the room. Behind her, Marat cried out in a strangled voice, "Help, help, dear friends." Simonne rushed to his side, but it was only to find his eyes glazing in death. Outside, one of his servants, alarmed by the outcry, felled Charlotte with a chair and pinned her down while others rushed off to fetch the police. This was hardly the ending she had foreseen, but the sensation was everything that she could have hoped for.

Four days later, the carefully embalmed body of Marat was borne through the city streets to the gardens of the Cordeliers, where it was laid to rest. The funeral procession was turned into a public spectacle, attended by the deputies, the members of the Commune, and groups from the sections. The leaders of the Mountain were determined to make Marat a martyr, even though they had feared him almost as much as his enemies had.

Charlotte's trial began the next day before the Revolutionary Tribunal. Her fate was settled before she entered

ARCHIVES NATIONALES: PHOTO BULLOZ

Charlotte's last letter from prison is reproduced at left. In it she assures her father that her action has saved the lives of innocent victims. She ends by writing, "Shame results from the crime itself, not from the punishment." According to one witness, she went to her death serenely (right), leaving "a memory of great courage and great beauty".

the courtroom, but she bore herself with dignity. "I killed one man," she replied to her accusers, "in order to save a hundred thousand."

The following day she went unmoved to her death. At the scaffold, the executioner tried to shield her from the sight of the guillotine, but she brushed him aside with the comment, "I've never seen one before. In the circumstances, I'm rather curious."

Charlotte Corday died in the belief that she had saved France. In fact, all she had done was to cut off one of the heads of the many-headed beast that was the Mountain. Marat's death strengthened the position of those who remained; they made him into the innocent victim of the Girondists. And with the removal of Marat, Robespierre was the undisputed leader of the Mountain. Only Danton was left to challenge his supremacy, and even Danton was no longer a serious rival.

The old leader of the Cordeliers was under a cloud. Early in 1793, as leader of the first Committee of Public Safety, Danton had begun to bargain with the Allies in the hope of making peace. Although his efforts failed, they

MUSEE LAMBINET, VERSAILLES: PHOTO JOSSE-LALANCE

received wide popular support. The French people were weary of war. But in the Convention, the deputies of the Mountain, now they were in power, were in favour of the war. Only while the fighting continued could they maintain the emergency forms of government that gave them their strength. They began to regard Danton's negotiations with suspicion, and his followers began to desert him.

Robespierre, once he saw which way the wind was blowing, also broke off his association with Danton. Although for the sake of appearances he made several half-hearted speeches in Danton's defence, he had no intention of sharing his old ally's disgrace. On July 10, Danton and the moderate Centre members of the Committee failed to win re-election, and their places were taken by extremists of the Mountain, including Robespierre's disciple Saint-Just and the crippled Couthon, another admirer. And on July 27, Robespierre himself joined the Committee, taking the seat of an unimportant member who had conveniently fallen ill. The fortunes of the Revolution were now in Robespierre's hands, and a new régime—the Rule of Virtuc and Terror—was about to begin.

MUSEE CARNAVALET

This moonlit scene of prisoners arriving in the courtyard of the Conciergerie prison during the Reign of Terror (1793–94) was painted by Polignac.

VII

THE TERROR

The Girondists, fulfilling the purpose for which they had been re-elected, introduced a new republican constitution to the Convention in February, 1793. Typical of its authors, it was worthy, wordy, and unworkable. The debate on its 368 articles went on despite the strife between the parties and was dragged out endlessly both by the long-winded speeches of the Girondists and by the delaying tactics of the Mountain. When the Girondists fell from power, only six of the articles had been discussed.

The Mountain hastily produced its own constitution, which was presented in June and rushed through the Convention in two weeks, before all of the deputies had even had time to read it. It was both briefer and more liberal than the Girondists' code, but many gaps in its provisions showed how quickly it had been drafted. However, the Mountain excused its deficiencies by pointing out that the Convention could fill in the details at its leisure. In any case, the Mountain had no intention of releasing its hold on the complex and interlocking machinery of the emergency war government that had been created in the early part of the year: the Committee of Public Safety, the General Security Committee, the watch committees, the deputies on mission, and the Revolutionary Tribunal.

Although the Committee of Public Safety was supposed to work with the ministers, it soon replaced them and became the executive branch of the government. It also issued decrees that a frightened Convention voted into law. By the end of 1793, the only government agency free of the Committee's control was the General Security Committee, which controlled the police. With this exception, the twelve men who formed the Committee of Public Safety and who were elected and re-elected to their posts by the deputies for twelve consecutive months, were the temporary rulers of France.

These twelve were an ill-assorted group. Coming from

vastly different backgrounds and from widely separated parts of France, they were bound together only by their ability, their dedication to the Revolution, and their ruthlessness. Yet while they held power they showed a remarkable unity of purpose.

They worked long and hard in their offices in the Tuileries, and it was a rare occasion when the Committee was not in session. No one presided over their meetings, and formally they had no leader. Nor were any of the twelve assigned to special duties, although by silent agreement they split the tasks of the government between them. The army was the special concern of Lazare Carnot, who had served as a captain of engineers and was the author of several brilliant military works. He was backed by Claude Prieur, also an engineer, who organized the manufacture of arms and munitions, and by Jean Baptiste Lindet, who proved to be an excellent quartermaster-general. Naval matters were handed over to Jeanbon Saint-André, an ex-merchant mariner who had become a Protestant pastor before espousing the Revolution. Another Prieur, called Prieur of the Marne to distinguish him from Carnot's colleague, handled finances, and the easy-living ex-aristocrat Hérault de Séchelles, the man who had drafted the Jacobin constitution, concentrated on foreign affairs when he was not absent on missions. The last two to be elected to the committee, Collot d'Herbois, a successful playwright, and Jean Billaud-Varenne, a lawyer and pamphleteer, were Parisian sans-culottes and had been appointed to avoid a clash with the Commune. To silence them, they were kept away from Paris by frequent missions to the provinces, where their violent policies could be used to the government's benefit. The shifty Bertrand Barère acted as the Committee's spokesman in the Convention, explaining its policies and steering its decrees to a favourable vote.

The one man who could claim to lead the Committee was Robespierre. With his disciples—Louis Antoine de Saint-Just, the pitiless and terrifying young man who was soon to earn the title Angel of Death from his colleagues, and the crippled lawyer Georges Couthon, who was confined to a wheelchair by paralysing meningitis—Robespierre shaped the policies of the twelve. He was by far the best known and the most influential member of the Committee since he had a large following among the deputies, the members of the powerful Jacobin clubs, and the sans-culottes of Paris. And, unlike the others, he never left Paris on missions and so was able to attend every meeting of the

MUSEE CARNAVALET: PHOTO GIRAUDON

Even for the members of the Committee of Public Safety, survival during the Terror was perilous. Above is Maximilien Robespierre, who, more than any one member, could be called the Committee's leader; born in 1758, he was executed in 1794. He is flanked by two men of less prominence but longer lives: at left is the clever lawyer Bertrand Barère (1755–1841); at right, the indefatigable military engineer Lazare Carnot (1753–1823). Standing jauntily at left, below, is another Committee member who outlived the Terror, but barely, the popular and outspoken actor Jean Marie Collot d'Herbois (1750–96). And to the right of Collot is his colleague Jean Billaud-Varenne (1756–1819), a lawyer so insatiable in his hatred of anti-revolutionaries that he finally attacked Robespierre as too "moderate". Beside him is the wealthy, cynical Hérault de Séchelles (1759–94), whom Robespierre succeeded in having guillotined. At right, below, is a young man of wholly different stripe, Louis Antoine de Saint-Just (1767–94), who worshipped Robespierre and accompanied him to the guillotine without complaint. Although brief, the association of these men and the other Committee members was dynamic and terrifyingly effective.

Committee during the first nine months of its career.

Robespierre had risen to power by sheer effort and concentration. He lacked the intelligence of a Mirabeau or the fire and passion of a Danton, but he made up for these deficiencies by a talent for hard work, a recognizable moral purpose, and a driving ambition. His narrow, bony face with its sharp nose and cold, blank green eyes had been prominent in all the debates since the beginning of the Revolution, and his primly neat figure could be seen hurrying from the Assembly to the Jacobin Club and back again at all hours of the day and night.

Known as the Incorruptible because of his unswerving honesty and rigid standards, Robespierre had one major failing: he believed in ideas rather than in men. He had never been forced to work with his hands or to face poverty

Under the Law of Suspects, which was passed early in the Terror, anyone who seemed to favour enemies of the Revolution could be arrested. This watercolour from that period shows three fédérés *making a street arrest as citizens gape. One of the guardsmen menaces the victim with his bayonet.*

or starvation, and he was out of touch with those who had. Although he was the champion of the people's rights, he never really understood their needs and their ambitions. He demanded from them a dedication to the principles of the Revolution, and he was dismayed to find that they were more interested in food and better wages.

Robespierre was not an original thinker. His gospel was the work of Rousseau, and his faith in the philosopher was blind. He swallowed the good ideas with the bad, the noble with the ridiculous. He believed that the people were good and true at heart, and he attributed their failure to follow his narrow-minded policies to the work of foreign agents. The idea of a foreign plot obsessed him, and he saw himself surrounded by spies and plotters and traitors. At last, anyone who disagreed with him became a traitor,

MUSEE CARNAVALET

and he set out on a fatal attempt to destroy those who opposed him.

Most of his colleagues agreed with him that if they were to succeed in preserving the "public safety", force—or terror, as they called it—would be necessary: their watchword was "Let terror be the order of the day." With ruthless determination, they began to hack their way through a jungle of problems by the use of intimidation and violence. With the Terror, they imposed their will on the French nation.

MUSEE CARNAVALET: PHOTO BULLOZ

The Girondists' mismanagement had left France in a desperate situation. The British blockade of the ports had reduced the country almost to a state of famine, and trade and industry were at a standstill. In the west of France, the rebels of the Vendée had won several victories and were besieging the town of Nantes on the River Loire. In the north, the army, demoralized by the desertion of Dumouriez, had retreated to a line of fortresses along the Belgian border and was being hard pressed by the Allies under Coburg.

And in Paris itself, the situation was no better. The Commune had fallen into the hands of the extremist *enragés*, who were the most violent of the sans-culottes. Led by Hébert, they demanded price controls and strong measures against food hoarders and speculators who were driving the value of the assignats further and further downward.

Fresh troubles faced the Committee after the escape of the Girondist leaders. The fugitives scattered into the provinces and raised the standard of rebellion. Normandy, and the districts around Bordeaux and Lyons were soon in revolt and were quickly joined by the city of Marseilles and the important naval base of Toulon on the Mediterranean. Here, royalists took control of the uprising and surrendered the town to Lord Hood, the British admiral in the Mediterranean.

The Committee took swift action against the rebels. Its troops quickly subdued Normandy. Marseilles was surrendered by its garrison after the rebel leaders failed to enlist the aid of Lord Hood. Toulon, which had been manned by a force of 17,000 Allied troops, held out longer.

In the propaganda print opposite, a victim is dispatched with "swiftness and decency" by the guillotine. This efficient but scarcely humane instrument (a model of which is above) came to be the symbol of the Terror.

It fell at last when a young artillery captain named Napoleon Bonaparte forced Hood to beat a hasty retreat under the threat of his cannon. Lyons saw the most bitter fighting of all. The town was at length battered into submission by the cannon of the Jacobin commander. Finally, regular troops shattered the Vendeans in a series of fierce battles that lasted from September until Christmas.

Each of the Committee's armies had been accompanied by a deputy on mission, who directed its assault. As each stronghold fell, these commissioners set up special courts to try the rebels, bringing the Terror to the rebellious provinces. Hundreds were executed at Marseilles and Toulon. At Nantes, nearly two thousand Vendeans were drowned in the river. Lyons suffered a fate as bitter as its resistance. Over fifteen hundred were condemned to death, and when the guillotine proved too slow, the victims were slaughtered by firing squads and blown to pieces with cannon. Many of the houses that had survived the bombardment were ordered to be torn down, and the name of the city was replaced on the maps with the grim word *sansnom*, "city of no name".

Meanwhile, in Paris, the Terror was sweeping up the remnants of previous régimes. In August, the queen was taken to the Conciergerie prison and finally brought to trial in October before the Revolutionary Tribunal. Aged by her imprisonment, her hair turned white by her misfortunes, she went to the scaffold unrepentant on October 16. The Duke of Orléans and the imprisoned Girondists, including Madame Roland, followed her soon after. Roland, still at large, stabbed himself to death when he heard of his wife's execution, and several other fugitive Girondists committed suicide to escape capture. Even the royalist ex-mayor of Paris, Bailly, was dragged from his retreat in the country and executed. The twelve seemed determined to make a clean sweep of the survivors of the early Revolution.

To speed up the work of the Revolutionary Tribunal, it was divided into four courts, which sat day and night. And in September, the flow of victims was swelled by the Law of Suspects, which increased the number of offences that could be tried by the Tribunal. Prisoners were tried in batches up to fifty in number, and justice became a mockery. Aristocrats, priests, hoarders and swindlers, common criminals, spies, and unsuccessful generals—even some entirely innocent victims—passed before the judges in droves, and the execution carts, the infamous tumbrels, rumbled along the streets every afternoon. Some of the victims had

MUSEE CARNAVALET: PHOTO BULLOZ

Marie Antoinette, hated by the French people during most of her reign, won admiration at her trial by her composure. This sketch of her at the prisoner's bar was made by F. L. Prieur, who was seated in the jurors' box. Prieur, who recorded many of the cruel events of the Revolution, was himself later executed for his inhuman attitudes.

been denounced by malicious neighbours or personal enemies; some were tried on flimsy charges. Innocent and guilty, young and old, men and women, over 2,500 of them went to the guillotine in Paris alone during the Terror.

The watch committees, which controlled the local Jacobin clubs, proved to be enthusiastic and hard-working agents of the Terror. They ferreted out suspects in thousands. They turned the provinces into a nightmare of fear, bloodshed, and destruction. In some areas, the anti-clerical attitude of the Jacobins became open atheism, and a crusade was waged against the Church. Priests were denounced and imprisoned, and churches were looted and defiled. Even Couthon and Saint-André, who had been sent to the provinces on missions of revenge, returned to Paris disgusted with the excesses of their provincial colleagues.

The atheistic movement found a natural home in Paris among the extremists of the Commune. They were en-

LOUVRE: PHOTO BULLOZ

ARCHIVES NATIONALES: PHOTO BULLOZ

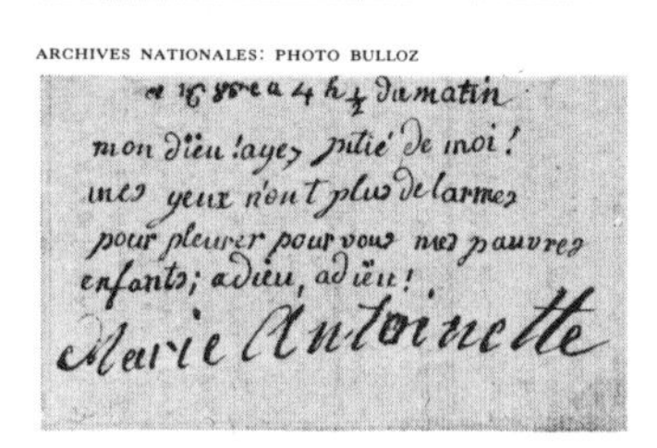
ce 16 8bre a 4 h ½ du matin
mon Dieu! ayez pitié de moi!
mes yeux n'ont plus de larmes
pour pleurer pour vous mes pauvres
enfants; adieu, adieu!
Marie Antoinette

On her way to the guillotine, Marie Antoinette (top) looked grim but straight-backed to the artist David. In her last note to her children (above), she asked for their pity.

couraged by the anti-clerical mood of the Convention. In September, the deputies reduced bishops' salaries, and in October they forbade the clergy to teach in the schools. In an even more striking move, the calendar was reformed. On this radical and colourful calendar, seven-day weeks were replaced by ten-day weeks, and the days were given numbers instead of names. Sundays, saints' days, and religious feasts all disappeared, and even the names of the months were changed to titles suggesting nature and the seasons—"windy month", "seed-time month", and so forth.

The sans-culottes went much further. In Paris, they closed all the churches in their sections. The Commune forced the Bishop of Paris to resign, and later in the year, it took over the Cathedral of Notre Dame for an atheistic Feast of Reason, during which busts of Rousseau and Voltaire replaced the statues of the saints.

Robespierre was shocked by these developments. They contradicted his theory that the Revolution was based on a belief in a Supreme Being and was rooted in moral virtues. Also, from a practical point of view, he realized that unless the atheists were checked, the Catholics would be angered and France would also be disgraced in the eyes of the world. However, in launching his attack on the atheists he could not admit that the movement had been started by French citizens. When he arose to speak on the subject at the Jacobin Club, he denounced it as a foreign plot designed to discredit the Revolution. He called on the club to purge itself of anti-Christians and extremists.

The charge of conspiracy, however sincere, served a second purpose; it also allowed him to point an accusing finger at the Commune, which was proving to be as troublesome for Robespierre as it had been for his predecessors in power. There could be only one government in France, and he was determined that it would not be the Commune. If necessary, he would use the weapon of the Terror against his own supporters.

While Robespierre was preparing to bring down the leaders of the Commune, Carnot and his colleagues were labouring to save France from military disaster. By August, they had the situation well in hand.

Carnot called for a general mobilization of all able-bodied citizens to fill the ranks of the armies in the field, which had been badly thinned by casualties and desertions. Soon, he had over 600,000 eager recruits at his disposal. Since there was little time to train them, he spread them out among his seasoned veterans and developed new mass tactics in which their sheer weight of numbers made up for their lack of experience. He also raised the sinking morale of the troops by replacing their aristocratic commanders with trustworthy revolutionary officers.

At the same time, Lindet and Prieur had completely reorganized the supply system of the army. New factories were set up to manufacture muskets and gunpowder. Church bells were confiscated to be melted down into cannon. Crops were earmarked for military use, and prices were fixed. Before long, material was flowing steadily toward the front to back up Carnot's efforts.

Carnot himself took over the direction of the campaign. His hard work had provided France with an army large enough to swamp her enemies, and the enemy provided him with a golden opportunity for victory. Coburg, the Allied commander, had besieged the frontier fortress towns of Condé and Valenciennes and was planning a march south on Paris as soon as they had fallen. However, his English allies were more interested in taking the port of Dunkirk, and they marched west to besiege the town. At the same time the Prussians moved east, intent on capturing Alsace, which had long been a bone of contention between France and Austria. Coburg was left with only sufficient men to continue the siege of Condé, and he had to postpone his invasion plans (see map on page 95).

Carnot's generals moved swiftly to profit by the enemy's division. By flooding the country around Dunkirk, he brought the English to a standstill and then forced them to retreat by circling around their flank. They fell back to Coburg's position in the centre. However, before they had time to settle in, Carnot moved his troops in a daring march across their front and outflanked the Allied lines once again. He drove in the Austrian wing at the village of Wattignies on October 15, the day of the queen's trial, and chased the invaders back across the French border.

Meanwhile, another French army had halted the Prussian drive in the east. Slowly, but surely, the Prussians were forced back, and by the end of 1793, French troops had once more taken the Rhine Province and had reoccupied the city of Mainz. Further successes were reported from the south, where Savoy was taken and an invading army of Spaniards was driven back across the Pyrenees.

By December, after only five months in power, the Committee of Public Safety had justified its policy of terror. Rebellion had been crushed and punished, the foreign invaders had been driven from French soil, and a measure

BIBLIOTHEQUE NATIONALE: PHOTO BULLOZ

BIBLIOTHEQUE NATIONALE: SERVICE PHOTOGRAPHIQUE

The queen's son is thought to have died in the Temple after the Terror. These contemporary drawings picture him being tormented by his brutal guard, Simon the cobbler.

MUSEE CARNAVALET

Robespierre staged a weird festival in honour of the Supreme Being in June, 1794. The feast failed to win many converts to the new religion, although this painting by Thomas Naudet shows an enthusiastic crowd surrounding Robespierre as he stands on the steps leading up to the statue of the Deity.

of peace had been restored, even if it had been won only by the sacrifice of lives and liberties. The twelve decreed a national holiday on December 30 to celebrate their success.

Yet success brought its own problems. Once the emergency had passed, the French people had time to concentrate on their old—and still unsolved—problems of food and money. Victories had not brought an end to their troubles, and the twelve had been too occupied with the war and the rebellions to do anything for them. Once again a rising tide of resentment and criticism began to beat

against the rulers of France. But the Committee had the means of silencing opposition, and it did not hesitate to use them against the people as they had used them against the enemies of the people. The Terror, instead of dying away, was intensified.

As always, Paris was the centre of the malcontents. Hébert and the *enragés*, who controlled the Commune and the sections, never tired of criticizing the leaders of the government. Daily they clamoured against high prices and low wages, food shortages and profiteers, the plots of the aristocrats and the priests. Robespierre for the first time became aware that his influence with the sans-culottes was waning. Now, the threat of violence was being directed against him and the Committee—and that was treason.

He and Saint-Just and their colleagues launched a smear campaign against the Hébertists. By slander and rumours, the belief was established that the Hébertists' actions were controlled by foreign agents and that their attacks on the government were plotted by the enemies of France. When the ground had been prepared, Robespierre's group moved into the open. In March, 1794, Saint-Just presented a report on foreign conspiracies to the Convention and succeeded in frightening the deputies into passing a law condemning anyone who criticized the government.

The following day, Hébert and several of his lieutenants were arrested. They were charged with conspiracy, and to give colour to the accusation, were tried with a group of foreign swindlers who had nothing to do with the extremist movement. They were given no chance to defend themselves. And on March 25, they went to the guillotine, leaving the sans-culottes leaderless and divided.

Robespierre had removed one danger to the government—and to himself—but another and more powerful threat to his position still existed. Danton was still alive, and while he lived, he stood in Robespierre's way.

After his beloved wife had died in the spring of the previous year, Danton had remarried and retired to his estate at Arcis to rest and relax. When he returned to Paris in December, he found that Robespierre was firmly in power and that the Terror, which he had favoured during the crises of the summer, was still in force. Always the practical democrat, Danton could see no further use for an emergency wartime government that ruled by violence. He scoffed at Robespierre's high-flown idea that the virtue of the people could only be achieved by wiping out the evil through blood. He knew the French too well; he understood that they wanted food and security, not virtue and self-denial. Rallying the moderates in the Convention, he called for an end to the Terror.

To Robespierre, Danton's leniency was as dangerous as Hébert's extremism. But Danton's popularity was an even graver danger to Robespierre's position. And the popular support for his views was a cause for alarm. The leader of the twelve decided that Danton and his followers must be removed if his own policies were to succeed.

He began his campaign once again by insinuations and rumors. When Danton was attacked by the Hébertists in the Jacobin Club, Robespierre rose to defend his rival; but

The Battle of Hondschoote, where the French troops flooded the lowlands around Dunkirk and defeated the English, is summed up in the drawing below. At centre, French wagoners halt and look over the scene of destruction as British forces retreat in the background.

BIBLIOTHEQUE NATIONALE: PHOTO BULLOZ

his defence took the form of a reminder to his audience of every offense—real and imaginary—which had been laid to Danton's account. By appearing to dismiss them, he was able to emphasize them, and he ended his speech with an underhand stab. "Danton," he said maliciously, "has always *seemed* zealous in the defence of his country."

Desmoulins took the sting out of this attack by accepting Robespierre's words at their face value. Reporting the speech in his new paper, *The Old Cordelier*, he linked Robespierre's name with Danton's as the leaders of the Revolution. However, in the second issue of *The Old Cordelier* he went too far for Robespierre. Desmoulins echoed Danton's plea for an end to the Terror under the headline "Open the Prisons". The article was aimed at the bloodthirsty Hébert, but Robespierre chose to see it as an attack on the policies of the Committee. He was also alarmed by the widespread support that it received in the Convention.

In the third issue, Desmoulins, excited by the attention his articles had received, went even further. He included a satire, supposedly translated from an ancient Latin writer, which described France under the Terror in terms of Rome in the first century B.C., when the republic was collapsing in ruins and Caesar was establishing his dictatorship. The comparison with Robespierre was unmistakable, and he retaliated at the Jacobin Club with a tongue-lashing that left Desmoulins pale and shaken: he knew that Robespierre never spoke openly against his enemies until he was fully prepared to destroy them.

MUSEE CARNAVALET: PHOTO BULLOZ

In this sketch of Danton on his way to the guillotine, the artist A. Witte shows the great revolutionary still untamed and derisive.

On the night of March 30, a joint session of the Committee of Public Safety and the General Security Committee, the combined executive power of the Revolution, witnessed the fall of a giant of the Revolution. Saint-Just laid before them a list of charges against Danton, which had been carefully drawn up by Robespierre, and called for his arrest. Some of the charges were true, many were ridiculous, but by morning, Danton and his associates had been taken to the Luxembourg prison. There, even with death staring him in the face, Danton found time for a joke. As he entered his cell he greeted the inmates with the wry comment, "Gentlemen, I had hoped to get you out of here. I'm afraid instead that I am to be shut up with you."

The trial of the Dantonists was an even greater mockery than that of the Hébertists. Once again, a batch of criminals had been mixed in with the victims in order to discredit them, but Danton's fiery eloquence was more than a match for such cheap trickery. He smothered the

Tribunal with ridicule and contempt in a voice that could be heard, it was said, on the opposite bank of the Seine. The public prosecutor, Antoine Fouquier-Tinville, fearing that his case would be drowned in this torrent of words, asked the Committee to silence Danton. Saint-Just went to the Convention with the story that Danton was preparing a revolt of the prisoners; he returned with a measure that forbade the Dantonists to speak in their own defence. The following morning, in their absence, they were condemned, and later the same day were carted off to the guillotine. Danton's last words were spoken to the executioner. "Show my head to the people," he said. "It is worth seeing."

Although the extermination of the Hébertists and the Dantonists left Robespierre without rivals for power, he soon appeared to be more insecure than ever. His fear of a foreign conspiracy became a nightmare, and an assassin's attempt on his life shook his nerve. The Committee's unity was shattered by a split over the execution of the Hébertists: Billaud-Varenne and Collot quarrelled with Robespierre over the destruction of the men who had been their allies. Meanwhile, Saint-Just and Carnot were at each other's throats over the conduct of the war. Robespierre began to believe that the safety of the Revolution lay in his hands alone, since he could trust no one else.

He sought to increase the strength of the Committee by systematically destroying the powers of the Executive Council, now a mere figurehead, the independent General Security Committee, and the Commune. The ministers were replaced with commissions elected by the Convention and packed with Robespierrists, while two of his supporters were pushed into the offices of mayor and district attorney of Paris, left vacant by the fall of the Hébertists. Finally, a police bureau was created to rival that of the General Security Committee. It was placed under the control of Saint-Just and later of Robespierre himself, who used it to weed out the deputies on mission who did not sufficiently favour his policies. Many of the deputies were recalled to Paris to be replaced in many cases by Robespierre's own followers. For some of them, recall was a death sentence, and the threat of execution hung over those who escaped.

Robespierre's manoeuvres finally forced his enemies to take action, but he was too engrossed with his plans to see the opposition taking shape. The deputies of the Centre, who had been cowed by the Committee's Terror, which could strike down a man of Danton's stature, were even

During the Terror, thousands of royalists escaped abroad, many to England. In this watercolour by Thomas Rowlandson, refugees are arriving at Southampton from the port of Toulon, where the Revolution fought one of its bloodiest battles against the royalists.

emboldened by Robespierre's distraction. Billaud-Varenne and Collot d'Herbois had a personal grudge to settle, and they were supported by Carnot, who resented Saint-Just's interference with his military plans. The leading deputies who had been recalled from the provinces by Robespierre —Fouché, Tallien, and Barras—went in daily fear of their lives; they dared not even go home at night.

United by fear, hatred, ambition, and the desire for revenge, these shrewd and ruthless men formed a con-

VICTORIA AND ALBERT MUSEUM, LONDON

spiracy to destroy Robespierre as he had destroyed so many of their friends and colleagues.

The plot came to a head in July. Disgusted with the failure of his colleagues, and exhausted by his labours, Robespierre retired to the country to consider his plans. His enemies used the time to perfect theirs. When Robespierre returned, they were ready for him, and blindly he played into their hands. On July 26, he appeared at the Convention and made a speech attacking his enemies and threatening them with the fate of all conspirators, but he refused to reveal their names. Confident of his strength, he played a malicious game of cat and mouse; he promised to return the following day and denounce his foes by name.

The next morning, the Convention was a scene of tumult. Deputies had to struggle to their seats through corridors crowded with sans-culottes and spectators. About eleven o'clock, Robespierre arrived, flanked by Saint-Just and Couthon, and took his seat among the deputies of the Centre, so as to be near the president's bench. Saint-Just went to the head of the assembly to lead the attack. Hardly had he begun to speak when Tallien pushed him from the platform. The young man's protests were drowned by the president's bell, rung by Collot d'Herbois, who held the important position on that day. One after another, the conspirators hurried to the platform to denounce Robespierre's followers and were rewarded with shouts of approval from the deputies.

Robespierre himself was thunderstruck. At last he rose and strode to the bar, but fury choked him, and he was unable to speak. One of the deputies howled, "The blood of Danton is choking him," and Robespierre too was pushed away from the rostrum. At last, the words came, but they were lost in the tolling of Collot's ominous bell. Then, amid the uproar, an almost unknown deputy named Louchet rose in his place and shouted, "I demand the arrest of Robespierre." The axe had fallen. The leader of the Committee of Public Safety was hustled from the chamber.

He was taken to the mayor's house, where word reached him that most of his supporters who had been arrested earlier had regained their freedom. They had gathered at the city hall and were appealing to him for guidance. But

A brilliant orator and a statesman of intense moral purpose, Robespierre was nonetheless vain and intolerant. Above is one of his vests, fit for a dandy; opposite, he is portrayed (by Boilly) seated proudly in his study.

Robespierre seemed paralysed. While he hesitated, the crowd of armed men summoned by the Commune to free his imprisoned colleagues began to melt away. By the early hours of the morning, the square in front of the city hall was deserted, and the building was unguarded.

The Commune continued to issue frantic appeals to the sections, but the leaderless Robespierrists did nothing to help. They seemed stunned by the disaster that had overtaken them. In any case, the old loyalties of the sans-culottes had been destroyed, and their leaders had been swept up in the Terror. Now, less than half were for the Commune; the rest decided to stand by the Convention.

Meanwhile, the Convention, learning of the Robespierrists' escape, branded them outlaws. This was the last blow for Robespierre. He had, perhaps, hoped that, like Marat, he would be triumphantly acquitted of the charges against him, but now that hope was gone. Numbly he joined his few remaining allies at the city hall.

By this time, the Convention had taken decisive steps to recapture the outlaws. Six thousand men had been recruited from the loyal sections and placed under the command of one of the deputies, an ex-officer named Barras. They marched on the city hall, which was taken without a blow, and burst in on the Robespierrists, taking them by surprise. In the turmoil, Couthon, trying to escape, fell down a flight of stairs. Robespierre's friend, Lebas, blew out his brains. Robespierre, attempting to do the same, only succeeded in shattering his jaw with the pistol ball, while his brother Augustin broke a leg leaping from the window. Saint-Just alone was taken unhurt.

The battered and bloody party was taken back to the Tuileries as dawn was breaking. Robespierre, his smashed jaw bound in a rough bandage, was laid on a table in the familiar offices of the Committee. He was a ghastly sight, smothered in blood, his shirt torn open, his clothes covered with dirt. For six hours he was left there bleeding while the Convention debated his fate. At eleven, he and twenty-two of his followers were taken to the Revolutionary Tribunal to be handed over to the executioner. The streamlined machinery of the Terror worked as swiftly on its inventors as it had on their victims.

At seven o'clock that evening, the Robespierrists went to their deaths. When Robespierre's turn came, the executioner ripped the bandage from his jaw, and he shrieked with pain. Moments later, his head toppled into the basket.

Robespierre, the last leader of the Revolution, was dead.

After Robespierre was arrested, an attempt was made by the Commune to rally the sans-culottes to his aid. Appeals, like the one at far right, addressed to Robespierre's own Section of Pikes, were sent out to all parts of the city but failed to arouse the citizens. Robespierre was re-arrested and taken back to the Convention after shattering his own jaw in a suicide attempt. For several hours he lay bandaged and bleeding in the rooms of the Committee of Public Safety (right). Later the same day, he and his followers went to the scaffold (below).

BOTH: MUSEE CARNAVALET. PHOTOS BULLOZ

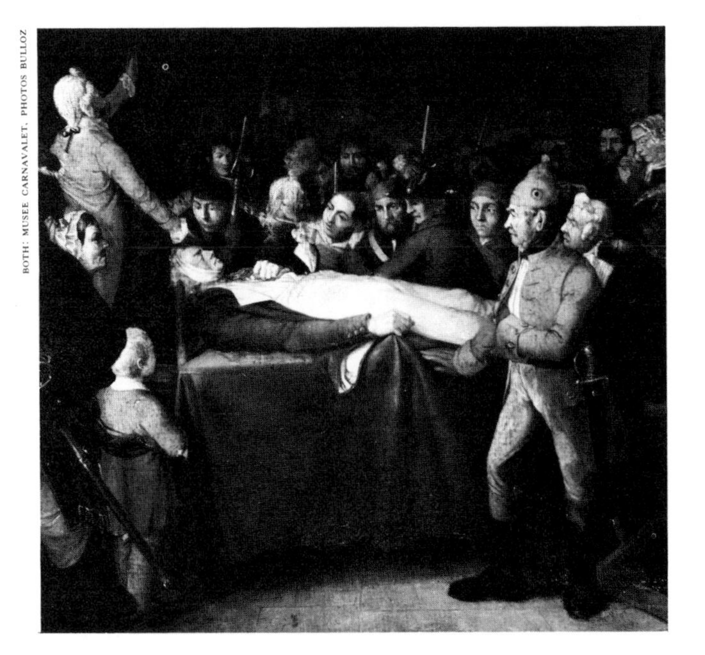

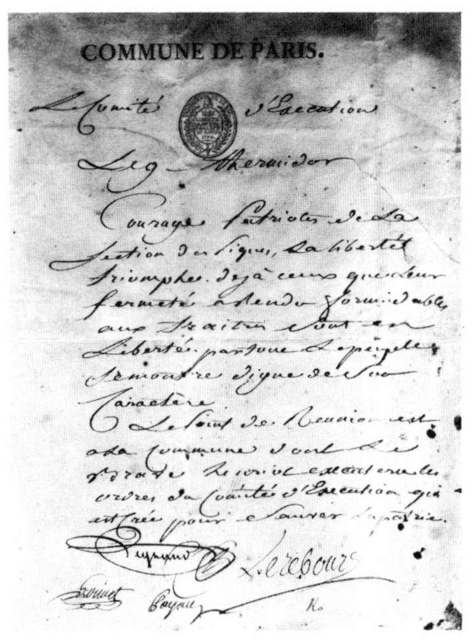

COMMUNE DE PARIS.

Le Comité d'Exécution

Le 9 Thermidor

Courage patriotes de la Section des Piques, la liberté triomphe. déjà ceux que leur fermeté a rendu formidables aux traitres sont en liberté. partout le peuple se montre digne de son caractère

Le point de Reunion est a la commune dont le brave Henriot executera les ordres du comité d'Execution qui est créé pour sauver la patrie.

Legrand Lerebours

Louvet Payan Ro

BIBLIOTHEQUE NATIONALE. PHOTO BULLOZ

VIII THE UNENDING

REVOLUTION

MUSEE CARNAVALET

A statue of Robespierre was never raised in Paris, nor is one likely to be. Just as he did to the revolutionaries of his own day, so Robespierre today represents a rigorous and peculiar point of view in the eyes of many who cherish French republicanism. It was he who wrote into law this phrase: "Any individual who usurps the nation's sovereignty shall be immediately put to death by free men." And it was he who on that basis was executed.

In a way, the Revolution seemed to end on the guillotine with him. Everything that he had built was quickly destroyed by the rebels who had overthrown him. Eighty Robespierrists from the Convention and the Commune followed him to their deaths within twenty-four hours. Then, at long last, the prisons were opened, and royalists, Hébertists, Dantonists, and other victims of the Terror were released. By December of 1795, the Girondists had been recalled to the Convention, and the Jacobin clubs had been closed. The situation was suddenly at a standstill.

The instruments of the Terror were also abolished or rendered powerless. The Committee of Public Safety was reduced to its former status of a committee of the Convention. The watch committees disappeared. The Commune was replaced by two committees, one in charge of the Paris police, the other handling taxation under the control of the General Security Committee.

Even the Paris crowd had lost its menace and its strength. Those sans-culottes who had once led it and organized it had been swept up in the Terror or in the purge of the Robespierrists. Without leaders, the Parisians were no longer an effective force. Two popular riots in the

Throughout France, "Liberty Trees" were planted to commemorate the Revolution. In this painting of such a celebration, a mayor (holding the shovel) is backed up by National Guardsmen and serenaded by singers and musicians.

BIBLIOTHEQUE NATIONALE: SERVICE PHOTOGRAPHIQUE

In this contemporary engraving, the Jacobin Club is closed as troops disperse the crowd. The motto over the door nevertheless reads "Unity, Liberty, Equality, a Republic Undivided, Brotherhood, or Death".

spring of 1795 were easily crushed by the National Guard, which was now under the control of the Convention. The rioters' cry for "Bread and the constitution of 1793" was ignored by the deputies, who were busy with their own petty squabbles.

However, the dismantling of the tools of the Terror left France without a working government, and the Convention was forced to draft a new constitution in 1795. It was based on a new theory put forward by Abbé Sieyès, who had survived the Revolution by retreating into the background. The executive was placed in the hands of a directory of five men, the legislature was divided into an upper and a lower house, and the vote was limited to property owners. Yet the Directory, as the new government was called, was no more successful than any of the revolutionary governments. The same problems of food shortages, rising prices, and falling assignats baffled the new rulers of France. If anything, the crisis grew worse as personal quarrels and party strife took up more and more of their time and attention.

The conservative royalist farmers of the Vendée finally capitulated to the Directory's armies. Here one Vendean signs a document of truce while others are given their weapons and return to their farms.

Even before the directors had been elected, events in Paris foreshadowed the troubles that lay ahead. On October 5, 1795, thousands of royalists joined with mutinous detachments of the Paris National Guard in a march on the Tuileries Palace to protest at the new constitution. Excluded from power by the new laws, they were determined to cow the legislature with violence, as the sans-culottes had done in the past. But now the deputies knew how to protect themselves; they were no longer afraid of the disorganized crowds. They placed the defence in the hands of Barras, the deputy who had commanded the troops that arrested Robespierre. Barras wisely called in the regular army and summoned the young Corsican artillery captain Napoleon Bonaparte, the hero of Toulon, to lead them. At the Church of St. Roche, not far from the Tuileries, Napoleon met the attack of the sections with deadly cannon fire —"a whiff of grapeshot", as he later called it—and within hours the rebellion was over.

The incident brought Napoleon into the limelight, and the sudden rise of this competent and ambitious army man scared the Convention. To rid itself of a possible military dictator, the Convention gave him command of an army and sent him to invade and plunder Italy. However, Napoleon increased his prestige with a string of brilliant victories and a successful campaign against Austria that forced the emperor to sue for peace.

Napoleon's sudden rise to prominence was but one of the Directory's troubles. The royalists had emerged from hiding, and many *émigrés* had slipped back into France after the fall of Robespierre. They brought a "white terror" to the south, with mass executions and prison massacres of Jacobins that recalled the savagery of the Committee's terror. At the elections, which were held after the approval of the new constitution, many of the old-time monarchists won seats, and their quarrels with the republicans in the legislature threatened the safety of the nation. To preserve the republic, Napoleon sent his tough lieutenant Angereau from Italy to occupy Paris and drive the monarchists out.

At last, Napoleon himself broke with the government.

BIBLIOTHEQUE NATIONALE: SERVICE PHOTOGRAPHIQUE

Soon after Napoleon took over the government of France as First Consul in 1799, he commissioned the magnificent portrait opposite from Antoine Gros. Less complimentary is the view above, by the English caricaturist Isaac Cruikshank, which shows Napoleon as a toy soldier fighting at Toulon.

MUSEE DE LA LEGION D'HONNEUR, PARIS

The militant glory and the unbridled terror of the French Revolution are captured in this dramatic sculpture, "The Marseillaise", by François Rude. It decorates one side of the Arc de Triomphe in Paris.

PHOTO, PIERRE DUBURE: AGENCE RAPHO

An expedition to Egypt, aimed at setting up a second French base against the English in the Mediterranean, had ended in disaster. British ships under Lord Nelson destroyed the French fleet at the mouth of the Nile and cut Napoleon's lines of communication. He had to abandon his army and slip back secretly to France.

His Egyptian campaign had the net effect of encouraging France's enemies to attack her once more. Both the Russians and the Turks, who had feared the appearance of the "revolutionary armies" in the eastern Mediterranean, now allied themselves with the English. And Prussia and Austria determined to renew their war against France's expanded borders. Napoleon, who had returned to Paris to explain the catastrophe to the people, found himself universally blamed, and he was denounced in the legislature. Furious, he summoned his troops, expelled the lawmakers, and took over the government of France on November 5, 1799.

He ruled the nation alone for the next sixteen years as a dictator, and it seemed as if his seizure of power had wiped out everything that the Revolution had achieved. Yet neither Napoleon nor the variety of rulers who followed him were able to erase the work of the men of 1789. The Revolution had changed France, and the French, irrevocably.

The motto of the Revolution—Liberty, Equality, and Fraternity—had become a reality. For although in the years that followed, liberty was sometimes suppressed, equality often applied to only a few, and fraternity constantly threatened by strife, these ideals still remain part of the Revolution's heritage to the French people.

The citizen of 1795 possessed freedoms that the citizen of the Old Régime could not have dreamed of. He was governed by an assembly that he had elected; he was served by courts in which justice was free and equal for all men; he could work when and where he liked; and he owed no dues and duties to the aristocrats. Although a definite class structure still existed in society, the peasant was as respectable in the eyes of the law as was the priest or the high-born. Most important, land could be bought and owned by anyone with the right price and the determination to work it.

Given these benefits, new generations of Frenchmen have gone on to win new freedoms for themselves and for the world. Indeed, in that sense, the Revolution can be said to have shown no signs of ever ending.

BIBLIOTHÈQUE NATIONALE: SERVICE PHOTOGRAPHIQUE

The privileges of the aristocracy and the Church, symbolized by weapons and mitres, are destroyed by four revolutionary threshers.

ACKNOWLEDGMENTS

The Editors would like to express their appreciation to the staff members of many private and public collections in which paintings, drawings, and articles of special importance to this book were found. Foremost among these collections are the Musée Carnavalet (museum of the city of Paris), the Bibliothèque Nationale, Paris, and the Musée de Versailles. In addition, the Editors wish to thank the following individuals for their assistance and for making available material in their collections:

Jacques Wilhelm, Chief Curator, M. Gallet, Curator: Musée Carnavalet

Jean Adhemar, Chief Curator, Cabinet des Estampes; Mme. J. Le Monnier, Chief Curator, Service Photographique: Bibliothèque Nationale

Marcel Bidault de l'Isle

Photothèque, Documentation Française

Special photography: Paris—Service Photographique, Bibliothèque Nationale; Raymond Laniepce; and Studio Josse-Lalance

Maps by Sean Morrison

FURTHER REFERENCE

Readers interested in viewing art and antiquities from eighteenth-century France will find exhibits of the period in the following museums and art galleries: the National Gallery, the Wallace Collection and the Victoria and Albert Museum, London; the Musée Carnavalet, the Bibliothèque Nationale and the Louvre, Paris; and the Musée de Versailles.

For those who wish to read further on the era of the French Revolution, the following books are recommended:

Brinton, C. *A Decade of Revolution, 1789–1799.* Harris L. Hamilton, 1935.

Castelot, A. *Paris: The Turbulent City.* Translated by D. Folliott. Barrie & Rockliff: Valentine, Mitchell, 1963.

Cobban, A. *A History of Modern France.* Vol. I, Penguin, 1961. *The Social Interpretation of the French Revolution.* Cambridge University Press, 1964.

Dowd, D. L. *Pageant-Master of the Republic: Jacques-Louis David and the French Revolution.* Lincoln, Neb., 1948.

Gershoy, L. *The French Revolution and Napoleon.* New York: F. S. Crofts, 1933.

Gottschalk, L. *Marat, A Study in Radicalism.* Allen & Unwin, 1927. *The Era of the French Revolution.* Boston: Houghton Mifflin, 1929.

Havens, R. G. *The Age of Ideas.* P. Owen, 1958.

Lefebvre, G. *The Coming of the French Revolution.* New York: Vintage Books, 1957. *The French Revolution.* Translated by J. H. Stewart and J. Friguglietti. 2 vols. Routledge & Kegan Paul, 1962, 1964.

Lewis, W. H. *The Splendid Century.* Eyre & Spottiswoode, 1953.

Loomis, S. *Paris in the Terror.* Philadelphia: J. B. Lippincott, 1964.

Mathiez, A. *The French Revolution.* New York: Grosset & Dunlap, 1964.

Palmer, R. R. *The Age of Democratic Revolution: A Political History of Europe and America, 1760–1800.* Oxford University Press, 1960, Princeton University Press, 1964. *Twelve Who Ruled.* Oxford University Press, 1959.

Pernoud, G. *The French Revolution.* Secker & Warburg, 1961.

Rudé, G. *The Crowd in the French Revolution.* Oxford University Press, 1959.

Stewart, J. H. *A Documentary Survey of the French Revolution.* New York: Macmillan, 1951.

Thompson, J. M. *Leaders of the French Revolution.* Blackwell, 1962. *Robespierre and the French Revolution.* EUP, 1952. *The French Revolution.* Blackwell, 1955.

Tocqueville, A. de. *The Old Régime and the French Revolution.* Translated by S. Gilbert. New York: Doubleday, 1955.

INDEX

Bold face indicates pages on which maps or illustrations appear

Finito di stampare nel mese di febbraio 1966 presso le Officine Grafiche Arnoldo Mondadori - Verona - Printed in Italy